KU-652-601

Mr Ray Would Like a Monkey

Mr Ray Would Like a Monkey

Memoirs from the Front Line of Humanitarian Aid

RAY TAYLOR

ORPEN PRESS

Published by
Orpen Press
Upper Floor, Unit B3
Hume Centre
Hume Avenue
Park West Industrial Estate
Dublin 12

email: info@orpenpress.com
www.orpenpress.com

© Ray Taylor, 2021

Paperback ISBN 978-1-78605-087-8
ePub ISBN 978-1-78605-088-5

A catalogue record for this book is available from the British Library. All rights reserved. No part of this publication may be reproduced, stored in a retrieval system or transmitted in any form or by any means, electronic, mechanical, photocopying, recording or otherwise, without the prior, written permission of the publisher.

This book is sold subject to the condition that it shall not, by way of trade or otherwise, be lent, resold, hired out, or otherwise circulated without the publisher's prior consent in any form of binding or cover other than that in which it is published and without a similar condition including this condition being imposed on the subsequent purchaser.

Printed in Dublin by SPRINTprint Ltd

This book is dedicated to my family: my wife, Liz, daughter, Jenny, and sons, Sam and David. Without their support there would have been no stories to tell

Acknowledgments

I would also like to acknowledge all the help that I have received from Orpen Press and my editor, Kerstin Mierke, as well as my friends who have given me feedback and suggestions: Ann Mulligan, James McCarthy, Geoff McAuley, Billy Gallagher, Michael Larkin, Cormac Mac Raois, Paddy O'Reilly and Anita Goodbody.

Contents

Phonetic Alphabet

There are many references in these stories to the phonetic alphabet. The International Radiotelephony Spelling Alphabet, commonly known as the NATO phonetic alphabet, is used widely in radio transmissions and uses code words for each of the letters of the English alphabet. The system is used so that critical combinations of letters or numbers can be pronounced and understood by those who transmit and receive voice messages by radio (or telephone), regardless of language barriers or the presence of transmission static.

The system is also used in many situations for the coded identification of personnel and locations.

26 code words in the NATO phonetic alphabet are assigned to the 26 letters of the English alphabet as follows:

A	Alpha	N	November
B	Bravo	O	Oscar
C	Charlie	P	Papa
D	Delta	Q	Quebec
E	Echo	R	Romeo
F	Foxtrot	S	Sierra
G	Golf	T	Tango
H	Hotel	U	Uniform
I	Indigo	V	Victor
J	Juliet	W	Whiskey
K	Kilo	X	X-ray
L	Lima	Y	Yankee
M	Mike	Z	Zulu

1

Miss Sarajevo

The questions that I am most often asked about being an aid worker are: 'How did you get started in this job?' and 'How can I get a similar job?' My stock answer to these questions is that in a moment of madness I volunteered, and you need to have a skill that is required. If you meet these criteria you can proceed to the next step and pick up the phone or go on the web. Additional training will be necessary in most cases for you to function in what will be a different culture and often dangerous circumstances. My experience is that, having had their questions answered honestly, most people will back off and give various reasons as to why they cannot leave home. They are tempted but prevented by life's everyday commitments, and it is difficult, if not impossible in most cases, to turn your back on home and family.

The job of an aid worker involves dealing with the disasters that can befall people, be it man-made disasters such as war, or natural disasters like a tsunami or earthquake. In some cases, both types are present and this can make the job just that bit more difficult – war and famine can occur simultaneously, or one can lead to the other. Apart from your specific qualifications, whether these are medical, engineering, logistics or whatever, it is essential to remain flexible and be able to work for long hours, in diffi-cult conditions and under pressure and retain a sense of humour.

People without a sense of humour make me nervous and I don't want them around me. Flexibility is paramount, as the situation can change from hour to hour or day to day.

Most aid workers will tell you that embarking on aid work was not a sudden decision but something that was bubbling away under the surface for many years. Eventually they reach the moment when they cannot resist the pull any longer. In my case, when I eventually picked up the phone and made the call, it was like a huge weight had been lifted off my shoulders. The imaginary guy sitting on my left shoulder who kept saying, 'Go on, do it,' had been let loose. He has now been running loose for over eighteen years and because of it I have been in many situations and places that I could only have dreamed about, had I not made the call – places such as South Sudan, Darfur, Bosnia, Afghanistan, Sierra Leone and many, many more.

However, it was a long time before I eventually got my first posting. With each refusal I felt more determined to do whatever was necessary to become acceptable to some aid organisation. They all wanted to know what experience I had in overseas work. As the answer was none, I was repeatedly turned down. I wondered many times how I could get the experience required if no one was prepared to give me a job. I was a 46-year-old businessman with a successful business in the construction industry and I wanted to share my expertise. But unless I was prepared to go overseas for at least two years, it seemed that I was of no interest to anybody.

It was in 1993 that the bubbles first burst to the surface, and I believe that two issues were instrumental in finally making me come to a decision. That year we bought an old house in Skerries, just outside Dublin. It was for us a dream house in a dream location. Almost a hundred years old, it was beside the harbour, and we set about renovating it with enthusiasm.

As luck would have it, just a few days into the renovation I suddenly had terrible pains in my chest. My wife, Liz, who is a nurse, realised something was wrong and rushed me to our local GP. What followed was the most frightening experience I have ever had (well, apart from Afghanistan, but that's a different story).

I was rushed into hospital, monitored and had all sorts of tests done. It took five days before the problem was finally diagnosed and I was very afraid during all of that time. During my first night in hospital I was in a high-dependency unit and could not even go the toilet without a nurse having to be close by – and I have a strange aversion to sitting on the toilet with the door open!

I lay in bed, terrified of falling asleep in case I would not wake up. As foolish as I knew this logic to be, I tried to stay awake. My thoughts were all over the place, but the main conclusion I came to was that I had worked hard, built up a successful business and was now going to die. End of story.

'Well, that was a waste of time,' I said, unaware that I had voiced my thoughts out loud. The nurse nearby asked me, 'What was a waste of time?'

'I have spent all my life working hard and took time for little else and now realise that I got it all wrong,' I explained. 'If I had my life all over again, I would certainly do things differently.'

A few days later I had a visit from a doctor who told me the good news. I had no cardiac problems. The bad news was that I had a stomach ulcer. We had a long chat about my work and lifestyle, which was work, work and work and he just said, 'If you want to kill yourself go ahead, you've had a warning.' I was being given a second chance. I decided there and then that things would be different. I wasn't too sure how, but I was determined that life was going to change. The details could be worked out later.

I returned home and worked on renovating the house and we moved in a few weeks before Christmas. There is an annual swim for charity in the nearby harbour on Christmas Day, and after the swim a few of our friends came to visit us and we had some drinks and snacks. People were standing around chatting and in the best of spirits. My three children, Jenny, Sam and David, were watching *Top of the Pops* on TV when the song 'Miss Sarajevo' by U2 and Pavarotti was played. The song had been recorded as a fundraiser for the charity War Child, which provides aid for children affected by war. As I watched the video, which depicted scenes from war-torn Bosnia, and listened to the haunting tune, I had a moment of epiphany when I realised what I wanted for my new lifestyle. I could envisage spending part of my time as an aid worker, and there and then I decided I wanted to work in Bosnia. I wanted a job where the issues involved were about people rather than money. U2 have a lot to answer for.

I was a bit worried that if I spoke about my newfound idea people would decide that I was cracking up and so initially kept fairly quiet about it all. I eventually discussed it with Liz and asked her what she thought of my suggestion. Her reply was very clear. 'If that is what you feel you should do, then go for it. Life is not a rehearsal, and you have only one life, so do the best you can with it'. I felt relieved.

In the new year I set about contacting various aid agencies and thought naively that it would only be a short time before I was on my way. This was not to be the case. I contacted the Red Cross, Goal, Concern, Oxfam and a few more. I filled in detailed application forms and the message back was that some of them were interested, but if they were to take me, I would have to commit to going overseas for two years, minimum. This was not at all what I had envisaged. I had thought that I could go for a month or two at a time and then work at my regular job in Ireland. Of course this plan was nearly impossible, as I could not walk off in the middle of a project – this was all a time of learning for me. I'd had an idea; I just hadn't thought it all through. But I wasn't ready to give up on it yet.

One day I bumped into a friend of Liz's who had worked in Africa and asked her for some advice. This started the ball rolling. She suggested that I make contact with a department within the Irish Department of Foreign Affairs called APSO, which special-ised in sending people overseas for short-term missions. APSO sent me an application form that I filled in and I subsequently went for an interview with a woman named Caragh. She would

Mr Ray Would Like a Monkey

turn out to be the key that would open the door for me into the world of aid work.

The interview was very interesting, in that it made me aware of various skills I had that could be of use overseas. I had tunnel vision when it came to what I thought I could do, but Caragh pointed out other skills I would not have considered relevant. For example, I had experience with VHF radios and first aid through my sport, motorbike racing. I never thought of this as an asset, but of course it was and I just needed for it to be pointed out to me. I was also used to arranging manpower and deployment plans for ambulances and crews at the motorbike races, and when this was combined with my managerial experience on building sites, the logistics box as well as the construction box was ticked. I was starting to see how I might be of some use after all on a mission but was still terribly naive as to what was required overall. Ignorance is bliss, until reality bites.

Later in the year an opportunity arose for me at home to take up a position as contracts manager for a specific job in another company and it occurred to me that maybe this was the way to go. If I was a freelance contracts manager, instead of running my own business, there could be times when a posting could come up and it might be easier to get away. So I chased up some freelance work. I was consciously making plans to free up time, but so far was not getting any overseas offers.

Then the long-awaited call from APSO eventually came. They asked me if I could go to Kenya to supervise the building of a school. However, as I had just started a new contract in Dublin for another contractor and this was to keep me occupied for over a year, getting away was not an option – but the thought of working overseas had not gone away. The offer yet again forced me to re-evaluate the way in which I was organising my work life, as the guy on my left shoulder was screaming that this was an opportunity lost. I agreed with him. Life seemed to be slipping back into the old pattern, even though I was now looking after jobs for other contractors. There were humanitarian emergencies occurring in various parts of the world, but I was still working in

Dublin and every so often pestering APSO with enquiries. I went to different meetings and discussions and heard about the experiences of other people, but it looked like I had missed the boat by not taking the job offer in Kenya.

It was now October 1997 and the war was officially over in Bosnia, but there were still security issues and the country was in dire straits. I was running a few small jobs in Dublin when I got the second long-awaited phone call from APSO. They had a request in for a logistician for Sarajevo in Bosnia. Would I be interested? At first I thought that the telephone call was a joke, and then I realised that it was a genuine enquiry.

My next thought was that I still had a few weeks to go before my existing contract was up, but then realised that it might be possible to leave, as the foreman in charge was completely up to speed on the jobs involved and the work was almost complete. I telephoned Liz and told her about the call from APSO and asked her what she thought about it.

'Well, this is what you've been hoping for, so make the most of it, but be careful,' was her reply. 'You have my blessing.'

I could have cried, I felt so relieved. We agreed completely, but I was very much aware that not many wives would be as supportive as Liz was. The contractor agreed to release me from my contract early and I accepted the offer from APSO and was told to be ready for a briefing in a few days. I was excited and terrified in equal measure.

Liz and I sat the family down and explained about the job, which was a short-term posting until December. The boys seemed to be OK about the whole thing, but Jenny expressed reservations. She had read somewhere that there were lots of landmines in Bosnia and that I would need to be very careful. This comment focused my mind. I then informed my mother and father, who seemed a bit shocked at the whole idea, but I was now in pre-departure mode.

I met with various people who had worked in Bosnia and was given some tips about security, unexploded ordnance and how to stay safe, as well as the type of clothing I would need for the

Mr Ray Would Like a Monkey

Bosnian winter. What they didn't tell me was what it was all going to do to my head, and how to deal with it all emotionally. I was about to start on a journey with a very steep learning curve.

2

Bosnia and Croatia, 1997

DEPARTURE

I completed my briefings in Dublin and was ready for the off. I was going to work for the OSCE (Organization for Security and Cooperation in Europe) Election Observation Mission and would be travelling alone, as all the other members of the team were already in position. I had a contact telephone number for the office in Sarajevo and had arranged to be met at the airport there.

It was not exactly working with starving people, which was what I had had in mind, but it was a start and at least I was going to the country that I had hoped to be working in. I was excited and couldn't wait to get going. At the same time I was quite nervous of what to expect and worried about being able to do the job. Nineteen missions later I am still the same way before I depart – excited, anxious, happy to be going somewhere new and sad to be leaving my family, a host of contradictory emotions.

Liz brought me to Dublin airport the morning of my departure and there was a tearful farewell as I began the first leg of the journey, to London. The next stage was London to Vienna but, due to a delayed departure from London, I was under pressure to make the connecting flight in Vienna. I just made it, with minutes to spare, but then the plane sat on the runway for some time. An hour or more later, we were informed that we had missed the landing window in Sarajevo for that day. It seemed that planes flying in and out of Sarajevo could only land and take off between midday and 3 p.m. and we would have been late for that slot. Instead we would fly to Split in Croatia, from where we would be bussed to Sarajevo. We were told that the bus journey would take approximately seven hours, most of it in darkness. I was somewhat anxious about this but felt a bit reassured that we were all in the same boat, so to speak. I used my mobile phone to inform the office in Sarajevo of the revised ETA.

CROATIA AND BOSNIA – FIRST IMPRESSIONS

Croatia was a bit of an eye-opener on my first visit, due to the number of military vehicles parked at the airport. The looks on the faces of many of the passengers indicated that this was new to them, too, and the few experienced people amongst us stood out at this stage. I, of course, was not part of that elite group. On the bus I sat beside a guy from the BBC and tried to pick his brains as to what to expect. I had some sandwiches that I shared with him (never travel anywhere without rations) and we drank water that had been supplied to us on the bus.

As we journeyed through Croatia, heading for the border with Bosnia, I could see in the twilight that the villages we passed through had been damaged during the war.

Roofs had been blown off houses and walls had been damaged by bullets or artillery. Some of the houses were occupied and candlelight flickered through the plastic sheeting that kept the elements at bay. My initial reaction was that it was not too bad overall, as many houses were actually in reasonable condition. I was to discover later that the religion of the occupants could be determined by the type of roof construction on the houses, which explained how some houses had little damage and others were in a very bad state.

However, as we neared Bosnia and then crossed over the border the scene became much worse overall. There had been a fair amount of chatter on the bus but as we passed through more and more scenes of destruction the chatter died down to a hush. Most of us were witnessing, for the first time in the flesh, what we had seen many times on TV. The reality has a horror that you feel deep inside but is very hard to explain. The expression 'shock and awe' is probably the best way of describing it. The sheer magnitude of the destruction, the bullet holes where houses had been raked with machine gun fire, left most of us in no doubt as to the destructive power that had been unleashed.

I knew from photographs that I had seen in tourist brochures that Croatia and Bosnia were beautiful before the war, but now the whole place was scarred. I realised just how sad it was to see houses that had been homes to so many families in such a terrible state. We journeyed on through the gloom and people started to doze off. Sleet was falling outside and conditions were not good. The driver had one cassette, which he played over and over until someone eventually lost their cool and told him to shut off the music. After that outburst we pulled into a small tavern for a toilet stop. Apart from that we had no other breaks. We were hours behind schedule because of the weather and at times I wondered if we would reach Sarajevo that night, but eventually around midnight we slithered into the city.

THE WOUNDED CITY

A city without electricity already has a sinister feel about it. When there are armoured personnel carriers and tanks parked around, a blacked-out city does not have a welcoming feel to it at all. The bus pulled up near the Holiday Inn, which I immediately recognised from seeing it on TV. Fergus, the guy from the BBC, offered to get me a bed for the night in the house where he was to be based, but I thanked him and went looking for my contacts. Obviously we were hours late and with no communication possible (my mobile had not worked since Split) my chances of making contact were slim, as I only had the office contact details. I learned from this experience, and now always have lots of different contact details when I travel to a new posting. There was no one there to meet me, but the bus had stopped at one of the few hotels that were doing business in Sarajevo.

My next lesson occurred when I went to book a room in the hotel. Accommodation is very expensive in war-torn areas and my credit card was of no use, as cash was the only way of paying bills. Currencies accepted were US dollars or Deutschmarks. You learn something new every day. I had brought US dollars with me as backup, which was what had been recommended during my briefings, and I was thankful for the information. I had a look around the reception area and could see where bullets had ricocheted off the walls and left some scarring, but then smiled as the night porter said, 'Welcome to the Holiday Inn, Sarajevo.' I was expecting Basil Fawlty to jump out next, so I suppose my tiredness was getting to me. It was a case of laugh or cry, so laughing seemed the best option. I would love to be able to say that I slept soundly, but sleep did not come easy.

First day

The next morning I was up, dressed and outside early to look at the city in daylight. I suppose I was a bit like someone who had just observed a serious accident – I was finding it hard to accept what I was seeing. The Holiday Inn had been repaired many times and so was not in that bad a condition, but the surrounding buildings were damaged to varying degrees. The Ericsson building nearby was a high-rise office block where most of the windows had been blown out! I heard the eerie sound of Venetian blinds rattling in the offices as the wind blew through them. Even now, many years later, if I hear Venetian blinds being rattled by a breeze, I find the sound very unpleasant. I telephoned the office and was collected shortly afterwards. It turned out that the office had checked on my progress and been told that the bus would stay overnight in Split, which was why no one had met me. Still, I was in Sarajevo now and was keen to meet the rest of the team.

I was introduced to the logistics unit, which consisted of a retired Irish Army Colonel (Mike), two British Army personnel (Miles and Julian) who had retired early, a retired German Air

Force pilot (Heinz) and a local logistician (Dragon). The first duty in this type of set-up is to have the security briefing. They can't have you doing the wrong thing and getting yourself blown up, so the morning consisted of several hours' briefing on potential dangers, how to make mayday calls on the VHF radio and all the various SOPs (standard operating procedures).

Mike outlined what we were required to achieve. The bottom line was that there were going to be elections in a matter of weeks and international observers were coming in from all over Europe to observe and report on the elections. Our job was to prepare the master plan for gathering up the observers, arrange accommodation in various locations, provide transport to make all this work and liaise with the military for adequate security. We had to factor in what could go wrong and have backup plans to overcome potential problems.

One of the many jobs of the OSCE was to ensure that elections could take place and our job was to ensure that the observers could confirm that all requirements had been met – or not met, if that was the case. It was at this time that I started to realise that I was not well equipped for a lot of the work involved, and while I might have been in charge of building sites in Ireland, this was a different story altogether.

RADIO TRAINING AND IT ISSUES

I had experience of using VHF radios, but not of official radio speak and procedures. I suppose it was a bit like someone being able to drive a tractor in a field but not knowing the rules of the road – a bit dangerous! My identity (ID) call sign was OD 020 and when I did a training mayday call I first identified myself as OH DEE OH twenty. Luckily enough I was not actually transmitting. I could see the look of horror on the faces of the ex-military men around me as Mike patiently explained that my ID was in fact Oscar Delta, zero two zero.

I had to admit that it sounded much better than OH DEE OH twenty. I was given a copy of the phonetic alphabet and told to

Mr Ray Would Like a Monkey

learn it fast, and that more tuition would follow. Keep up here, lad! The next hiccup, however, was just around the corner.

A laptop was placed on my desk and I had to explain with much embarrassment that my computer skills were, to be honest, non-existent. I had spent all my time up to now either drawing building details for clarification, or having secretaries type up information I had put together into presentable form, so it was the typists who had the computer skills, not me. This looked like a problem and I was worried. I had a chat with Mike, who decided that, as a large part of our work would be out checking accommodation, arranging schedules and liaising with the military for security support, some of this work could be undertaken by me. Heinz was looking after the logistics for a separate group of observers, these being the members of various European parliaments, and the plan was that I would work as an assistant to him. Now that it had been established just how little I knew, I was slotted into plugging the gaps.

LIVING QUARTERS

The next issue was to find accommodation. One of the local drivers had details of what was available and I set off with him. I was relieved to be doing something that I knew I could cope with. I was offered a room in a tower block in an apartment that was owned by a local shopkeeper. The block was a few miles from the office and it too had been hit by shellfire, but had been patched up with some plastic sheeting while the long-awaited glass was on order.

I was immediately struck by what opportunities existed for a businessman to make a fortune setting up a glazing company and had to kick the idea out of my head. I was trying to leave all that behind, but old habits die hard.

The owner of the apartment was called Farouk and could not speak a word of English.

I could not speak a word of Serbo-Croat so it looked like there might be some communication difficulties, or 'comm probs', in the new language that I was learning. The driver acted as interpreter and we agreed rent and general terms. I had my own bedroom and could use the rest of the apartment, bathroom, kitchen, living area etc., which was shared with Farouk.

There were lots of candles around and the driver explained that electricity was in very short supply and that different parts of the city had electricity at different times, but that there was no agreed schedule, so you never knew when to expect power. There were about three dozen large plastic Coke bottles lined up in the bathroom, most containing water, and he explained that these should be filled whenever there was water in the taps because there could be a long gap, sometimes days, when there would be no water supply. We needed to stockpile water, another lesson learned. When all the details had been explained, Farouk produced a bottle of brandy and wanted to toast the agreement. I declined, as I did not think they would be too impressed at the office if I came back on my first day reeking of alcohol.

TRANSPORT ARRANGEMENTS

Back at the office I was informed of the next day's plans, which involved checking out some of the locations where the observers would be based in a few weeks' time. I was to travel with Julian and start to get a feel for the place. I was to be at the office at 5 a.m. the next morning and was to be out 'in the field' for the day. I had to make arrangements for travelling to and from work, as the only means of transport were the trams or locals who used their cars to provide a taxi service, mainly for the internationals. I had the address of the apartment written down and the address of the office and planned to show this to the taxi drivers until I could get them to understand my (mis)pronunciation of the address.

When I arrived back at the apartment that evening, I tried the first of my many strange conversations with Farouk. These consisted of sign language, notes and much waving of arms on both sides. There was a place nearby where the local 'taxis' parked, but no one would be driving around at 4.30 a.m. looking for business. Later, when I got to know the place, I was able to walk to work, but during the first week or so, in the dark, it was quite tricky. Farouk eventually understood my dilemma, looking at my note with 'taxi' written on it and me pointing at the office address and indicating 4.30. He laughed and shook his head. I could imagine him thinking, 'Silly man'. Nowadays, of course, I would arrange for our driver from work to pick me up during the first few days until I knew where I was going, but I was new and did not want to admit to any more problems. I was resolved to sort the matter out some way or other by myself. Farouk pointed at himself, made the motion of driving a car and pointed at the note. Problem solved, he would bring me in and so I found myself standing at the office gates the next morning, waiting for Julian and our own driver to appear.

DAY 2

We spent the day visiting area after area and discussing various issues with the OSCE field staff. I could grasp what the overall plan was, but the minute details involved left me feeling like a fish out of water. Another item was mentally added to the list of training courses required when I got back home. As well as typing, computer training, radio and communication systems, security procedures, land mine and UXO (unexploded ordnance) aware-ness, I now had procedures for election observers to add to my ever-increasing list – and it was only my second day!

We did not return to the office until 7 p.m. that night or, more correctly, 1900 hours. There was a notice on the wall: 'Civilians call it planning, we call it logistics'. It summed up my situation. I was not speaking the correct language. I decided there and then that I had a choice when this trip was all done. Give up and go back to what I knew, or start learning. Going back was not an option. That decided, I felt that this on-the-job training was an opportunity not to be missed and so I set about asking questions and trying to build up some knowledge.

To be fair, the guys were very patient with their 50-year-old trainee, but it was very obvious to me that a lot of time would have to be spent when I returned home learning about a wide range of new topics. How to achieve this was another problem. For instance, as far as I knew, I could not go to night classes for dealing with unexploded bombs and ordnance, and the intricacies of getting out of a minefield in one piece were not advertised as optional extras alongside foreign language courses. The list got longer, but once you decide you are going for it, whatever 'it' happens to be, the challenge to succeed at something new can be invigorating.

Julian and I left the office that evening and went to meet up with some of the other team members for a meal and a few drinks. I was bit shocked at all that I had seen during my second day. As well as the damage to property, I had seen lots of areas taped off because of land mines, and a lot of the victims of the war.

LAND MINES

It seemed that there was a considerable number of amputees about. As bad as this was when the victims were adults, the injuries inflicted on the children were horrific. Those not injured by shrapnel and gunfire had in many cases fallen foul of the landmines. The landmines were literally everywhere. The standard rule was, do not walk on any soft ground. Because of this, grass verges on the roads, even in the city centre, as well as parks and gardens were no-go areas. Children playing football in a street could on occasion forget the problem, and when a football got kicked into a garden and they went to retrieve it, they could become innocent victims.

Every day, reports came in of landmine strikes, as they are called. One strange side effect was that car theft was very low. I heard that car owners left landmines around their cars at night in some areas and, with no streetlights to help them see, car thieves were not taking any chances.

In public places the mined areas were marked with metal plates depicting a skull and crossbones hanging on barbed wire and the word 'MINES' printed on the plate, or sometimes the areas were marked with black and yellow tape. Even now, when I see black and yellow tape used by contractors in Ireland I instinctively move away. Once learned, never forgotten.

NEW DRIVERS

The journeys up and down Bosnia continued, and I started to get a feel for the job. We were hiring over 40 drivers on short-term contracts so that the international observers would have transport at all times, and this involved interviews, checking driving licences, insurance papers etc. The drivers would be issued with OSCE number plates while they were on the payroll and so setting up the new drivers and vehicles took a bit of time. Nothing was left to the last minute.

One driver was middle-aged and seemed very suitable for the job. His papers checked out and we went to check out his car. It turned out to be an old but well-kept Mercedes with automatic transmission. This was an unusual luxury in Bosnia, as most of the cars were battered Fiats or Ladas. My landlord Farouk's car was probably 30 years old and most of the dashboard was missing, as was the case in most of the local taxis, so we were incredibly pleased with our find. We did not notice during the interview or afterwards that the driver kept his left hand in his pocket. A few days into his contract, one of the international staff came into logistics and asked us why we were hiring one-armed drivers. We were all puzzled until it was pointed out that the driver of the Mercedes had a prosthetic left arm and that he kept his left hand in his pocket most of the time. Now we knew why he had a car with automatic transmission. Another war victim adjusting to a different lifestyle. Miles, who had overseen the hiring the drivers, indicated that he was very happy with his driving and asked if anyone had a problem with us having a one-armed driver. No one did.

MASS, GUNFIRE AND THEN LUNCH

Sunday morning in Sarajevo was a time for catching up with people from Ireland. An English-language Mass was held in the

Catholic church in the city centre at midday and Mike had asked if I would like to go with him. I pointed out that I was Anglican but would be very happy to accompany him. Mike stuck his head around the door of the logs office shortly before midday on my first Sunday and enquired if I was ready. Julian looked up and enquired, 'Ready for what?' and we explained that we were going to Mass.

Julian had spent a lot of time with the British Army in Northern Ireland and remarked that he thought that Mike and I would prefer to kill each other rather than go to Mass together.

Mike just smiled and said, 'And that is why the English will never understand us.' A littler banter was OK, but sometimes a chance remark could hit a nerve.

We arrived and went into the church, where a lot of military personnel from different nations were already seated. Most of the military had side arms, but the Americans carried M16 rifles with the rifle straps over their shoulders and looked completely out of place. When they stood up or knelt down for the prayers, the rifles swung loose and banged into the chairs in front of them. When the priest stood up for the homily it all seemed surreal to me. Never in my wildest dreams could I have imagined being in this situation.

A few minutes into the homily the main door opened and a woman walked straight down the aisle towards the pulpit. She stopped and stared at the priest and I noticed that she held an exceptionally large handbag in front of her. She stood very still and I felt that the congregation seemed to be uneasy – or was it my imagination?

'What's in the bag?' hissed the guy beside me, and I felt even more uneasy.

There were two soldiers in front of us and slowly the rifle straps slid off their shoulders and their guns were brought to a rest over their knees. I thought that if there was a hand grenade in the bag and it went off, there would be a lot of damage and still I sat and watched, mesmerised. The priest droned on, but no one appeared to be listening to him. They were all watching

Mr Ray Would Like a Monkey

the woman standing in the aisle. My mother was deeply religious but also very conservative and did not agree with people going to what she would see as 'the other side's church'. The crazy thought struck me that she would be very annoyed if I got blown up in a Catholic church. I could imagine her saying that it was bad enough to be blown up, but blown up in a Catholic church – unforgiveable! Suddenly the woman turned on her heels and walked back towards the main door and left the church. I was sure I heard a collective sigh of relief.

We left the church and met up outside for a chat with some other Irish people, mostly military personnel. It was a cold, dry day and Mike and I decided to walk a short distance to get some lunch. There was a hotel nearby that had just reopened but was only doing lunch at that stage. They served delicious vegetable soup and bread and one or two other items on a very limited menu. We liked the soup and had agreed that this was just what we needed. As we walked across a small park we heard several shots ring out, followed by silence.

'Did that sound like gunfire to you?' enquired Mike. I agreed that was exactly what it sounded like and he just remarked, 'I hope that the soup is nice and hot'.

I was amazed at his reaction, but many years later when I was lying on the floor of a house in Darfur, caught up in crossfire, I commented that I hoped the kettle would not get hit as I was dying for a cup of tea! I too had learned by that time that it is good to focus on small pleasures when in difficult circumstances.

THE OBSERVERS

On election day each observation team (consisting of two people) normally covered an area of three separate zones and went from zone to zone several times during the day. The plan was that the observers would be in Bosnia for approximately ten days, first being briefed and then being placed near their observation zones around the country. After the elections they would be collected, debriefed and then would return to their various countries. Logistics were at this stage dealing with the latest information coming in from various countries concerning the identity, passport number and gender of the observers.

It was not always obvious from the names whether the observer was male or female and, as there would be room sharing, we had to make sure that observers of the same gender were roomed together. A few of the observers were due to come into Sarajevo overland, but the majority had to be met in Vienna. We planned to set up a temporary reception area for a day at Vienna airport and then gather them up and fly them out in the evening from Vienna to Split. Flying them directly to Sarajevo was considered and then rejected for a variety of reasons, including weather and because the security window was just too narrow. I was familiar with that problem.

SARAJEVO – SPLIT – VIENNA

And so, on a very cold Sunday morning, Julian and I headed by road from Sarajevo to Split, in Croatia. No visits to Mass that week. As we travelled through Bosnia we had to cross several Bailey bridges that had been constructed by the military engineers, as the original bridges had been blown up. These bridges were still guarded in case of attack and in several locations were guarded by Russian troops. The weather conditions were terrible, with sleet and high wind and I felt sorry for these very young men, some of them only teenagers it seemed, who were tasked with the guard duties. The cynics said that as the Russians were used to bad weather, they got all the bad postings. I found them to be very polite and good-humoured at all times and once again my eyes were opened to what people are really like. If you want to know what people are like, work and live among them and you will get the real story.

We arrived in Split and did the final check on the hotels, as we would be bringing the observers there for an overnight stay before bussing them on to Sarajevo. The first thing I did when I arrived in my room was jump into the hot shower. The lack of water or electricity in Sarajevo wasn't a problem for me except when it came to the cold showers, which I found difficult. In Sarajevo, the procedure for washing was to get a few Coke bottles of water, pour some cold water over the body and then, shivering, soap rapidly. Once soaping was complete came the next exciting bit: washing off with cold water. I enjoyed having the hot shower in Split and felt like a new man. The temperature in Split was a lot higher that in Sarajevo, with Split being at sea level, and it was wonderful to be near the sea again. We flew from Split to Vienna the next morning and arrived at our hotel near the airport, where another hot shower was enjoyed. We had to finalise the arrangements for the set-up in the airport for the following morning, and were given a desk in the arrivals area, just before customs. We placed a large sign on the desk: 'OSCE Observation Mission'. We hoped that in this way no one would escape into the main airport area before checking in with us first.

Vienna – Split – Sarajevo

We spent most of Tuesday checking people in at Vienna airport, telling them the travel plans and the number of the boarding gate for the charter flight, which was leaving that evening. Some wanted to know what it was like in Bosnia and Croatia and it struck me that this had been my situation just a few weeks earlier. Now I was settled in and sharing information, like I had always been doing the job. The day flew and we gathered up all our people around 7 p.m. to board the flight to Split. There were a few nervous laughs from the newcomers, who needed to be reassured that they would not be shot down on the way.

One hour later we arrived in Split, to be met at the airport by the military, as normal. I was starting to feel a lot more confident and was reassured that all the planning seemed to be working out. A lot more of our team had arrived during the day from Sarajevo into Split to meet the newcomers, and so we broke up into groups and brought the observers to the different hotels. This went without a hitch and afterwards Heinz and I went out for a meal in a restaurant near the harbour. I liked Heinz, he was good company and had a relaxed manner. My first few days had been very trying, what with everything being new and the emotional strain of seeing seriously injured people, but Heinz in particular had done a lot to help me settle in.

Early the next morning we gathered up our charges on the tour buses we had arranged and checked that we had not left anyone behind. The buses had been brought in from Austria by some astute business people, as most of the local buses in Bosnia had been destroyed. I was in charge of settling the hotel account. When I checked to make sure that we had been charged for the correct number of guests before signing off, I discovered that we were being charged for three extras. I had to spend some time checking the bills against our own schedule before we could identify where the problem was. Another branch of the OSCE had three guests staying in that same hotel and these were being charged to us as well. Once this was sorted, we were on our way to Sarajevo.

As we journeyed along I was able to observe the passengers in daylight as they looked out on the surrounding countryside. Their reactions were similar to what I had experienced on my initial journey from Split to Sarajevo. People remarked that the damage was not too bad as they chatted away to one another. However, when we crossed the border into Bosnia and the true nature of what war can do started to sink in, the atmosphere changed and the small talk died away and silence set in. They were shocked and a few shed silent tears.

Someone had written 'Welcome to Hell' on a house in Sarajevo and it certainly felt like it at times. We eventually arrived at the Wounded City, as it was now called, and the observers were brought to a hotel for an initial briefing, where the warning to not walk on the grass was mentioned once again.

We returned to the office but were soon on the move again. Several observers had travelled overland and our rendezvous point was in a place called Novo Sarajevo, which is close to the airport. It was my first time in this area, which was heavily mined, and I was very conscious of the danger all around me. I endeavoured to appear nonchalant about the whole business, but it is in fact quite stressful when you are first exposed to these sorts of conditions with minimal training. In later years, after I had completed several training courses with the army, I was still very much aware of the dangers but more reassured about how to deal with the situation. The same training would later save me from injury or death in Afghanistan, but now, I was somewhat rattled.

We met the last few observers who had travelled overland and delivered them to the main observer group, which had arrived earlier. The trip to Novo Sarajevo appeared to have had an effect on the rest of the logistics team. They had become very quiet, with hardly a word spoken, as if to talk would be sufficient to land us all in trouble. There was no joking or banter. Everyone seemed very down. For me, the constant presence of the landmines was generating a stress I was not aware of at the time. It only started to show when I came home and found that I could not get them out of my mind. On talking with other people who had been in the same sort of situation, I found that I was not unique in that regard. We cope with the situation at the time, but when it is all over many aid workers show signs of stress, or in some cases post-traumatic stress disorder. We discover that we are normal people who have been in abnormal situations and it takes time to adjust. Once that is accepted, life becomes easier.

INJURED OBSERVER

We received a call from the hotel where the observers were staying. One of the Members of Parliament from the EU group had fallen and injured her knee. I was asked to assess the situation and deal with it. I had advanced training in first aid and so was the person on call for injuries – at least I had some skills that were in demand. It turned out to be a minor injury that simply needed an ice pack and then strapping. As I was applying the strapping the MP asked where I was from and I answered, 'Ireland.'

'Oh, it must be great to be Irish,' she replied. 'Everywhere in the world where there is trouble, the Irish are there helping.'

I was pleased at this comment and felt a bit more reassured. I was making progress – slowly!

KING'S OWN HUSSARS

Now that the observation team had arrived we needed to book space and time for press briefings. The international press area was in an old army barracks in Sarajevo and space and time in the area was limited. A British Army Lt. Colonel was in charge of the barracks and all requests for time slots went through him. We had attempted to arrange times, but were still awaiting confirmation, and so I was dispatched to see what I could organise. I had enquired as to how I should address the gentleman involved and was told to call him colonel. I didn't want to cause offence by addressing him incorrectly. I thought that it would be better if some of the ex-military went to see him, but no one wanted to go. I met the colonel and we had a chat. He was quite dismissive when he found a civilian was there to meet him and told me to come back the next day. I could see why no one else wanted to be involved in making the arrangements. I had noticed epaulettes with the letters KOH on his uniform and enquired from Miles if this indicated the King's Own Hussars Regiment. Miles confirmed that this was the case and I filed that information away for future use.

The next day, when I travelled back to the barracks, I enquired politely of the colonel as to his shoulder insignia and asked if the insignia was that of the King's Own Hussars. Of course he said it was and I told him that I was so happy to meet him as my grandfather had been in the British Army and this had been his regiment. After that everything went smoothly. He asked me what dates and times we wanted for the press conferences and everything was agreed on. I was a happy man and returned to the office.

The team enquired how the meeting had gone, and when I explained that we had all the dates and times as requested, this caused a bit of a stir. I recounted my conversation with the colonel and Miles remarked that I was incredibly lucky that my grandfather had been in the same regiment, as otherwise we would probably have still been looking for the dates.

Mr Ray Would Like a Monkey

'It had nothing to do with luck,' I said, 'my grandfather was actually in the 4th Queen's Own Hussars and not in the King's Own, but sure I'm just a civilian, so how would I know the difference?'

I felt that I was starting to find my feet and that maybe the matter of my lack of computer skills would be forgotten for a while.

ELECTIONS

The observers were briefed and we dealt with queries as they arose, but nothing too difficult occurred. The observers' job was not complicated, as all they had to do on election day was check that nothing irregular occurred during polling time. To facilitate their reports they had been issued with questionnaires, where the only option to each question was yes or no. For example, one of the questions was, 'Did you see any intimidation at the polling booth?' and the observers had to tick the correct box. Based on the feedback from the observers, the elections could then be declared fair or otherwise.

The biggest problem was when the observers tried to fax in their report sheets using satellite phones, which was a fairly new technology at that time. The speed was too slow, and we had to resort to the tried and tested system of hand delivery. We had tested it, but not enough, it seemed. Another lesson learned – if you are going to use new technology, test it in several locations before approving it.

Before we knew it, the elections were over and we had to depart from Sarajevo to Split once again to get the observers to the airport there. We did not get away until lunchtime, as the observers were being debriefed before leaving. I again travelled in the bus with the EU MPs and now that everyone was so relaxed it was a very enjoyable experience, with lots of talk and laughter. We travelled in convoy and were motoring along near the edge of a deep ravine when I suddenly heard the roaring noise of a helicopter close by. It swept upwards from out of the ravine and flew alongside us. We were looked at carefully by the machine gunner who was strapped in at the doorway. He was awfully close to us, and as he stared at us I waved my arm in greeting. He smiled, then saluted me and shortly afterwards the chopper banked away, just as suddenly as it had appeared. A feeling of reassurance came over me then – someone was looking out for us. I realised that I was enjoying all this excitement. The addiction had started without me being aware of it!

SPLIT

We arrived in Split and I had a meal out with Heinz, after the obligatory hot shower.

The observers stayed overnight and early next morning we brought them to the airport for departure. It was a strange feeling, saying goodbye to people that I had only known a short time, and yet during the time involved we seemed to have become a very tight-knit group.

I noticed an RAF plane on the runway and a large contingent of soldiers getting ready to return home. I chatted with one of the soldiers, called Patrick, who turned out to be Irish and discovered that they were from the Royal Engineers and had been based in Banja Luca, a Serb area. While we were talking, a young woman came along to say goodbye to another of the soldiers. She was obviously sad to see him go and gave him a hug. I was struck by her good looks, but when she turned to leave I was shocked by the disfigurement on the other side of her face, which I had not seen when she had first passed by me. The left side of her face was horribly scarred from shrapnel, so that she looked like a different person. I felt like I had been punched after seeing the damage that had been inflicted on her. I walked away, suddenly feeling very subdued. Would I ever get used to this type of situation, I wondered? I have since discovered that you do adjust sufficiently to deal with these types, of situations but see it as normal? Never!

Mr Ray Would Like a Monkey

ZVORNIK

We travelled back from Croatia to Bosnia, this time by car. My time in Bosnia was coming to an end. We were starting to close down the Observation Mission and already some of the staff had departed. Business was slowing down and a few days later I was asked to travel to the Serbian border and meet up with some other OSCE staff who were based in Serbia, and to collect some accounts from them. I was informed that they would be travelling in a green car.

The meeting point was near a bridge outside the town of Zvornik, which is adjacent to the border. The actual border post was beside a bridge over a river and it was nice to be out in the countryside again. The road was very narrow and we pulled over to one side to park. I started to get out of the car to stretch my legs, but as I opened the door I realised that we were on the grass verge and I pulled my legs in abruptly. The warning – don't walk on the grass – was imprinted on my brain.

We moved the car so that we could get out on to the hard surface and waited for some time. There was very little traffic and when eventually a green car appeared around the corner I stepped out onto the road to greet the occupants. Big mistake, I realised at the last second, as the car narrowly missed me and continued on its way. Wrong car! Eventually our green car did appear, and we had a meeting with the team in their car. It only took a short time as it just involved me going through some accounts and getting clarification on some items. Once the details were sorted out, it was time to travel back across country to the office. It was a cold afternoon, but dry, and I enjoyed the trip back to Sarajevo. I was definitely more at ease than I had been in the early stages of the mission.

No photography allowed

A few days later I made my way from the office back to Farouk's to pack my bags. I was due to leave the following day. I passed by the Russian control point at the end of the road and waved as usual to the Russian officer, standing beside the huge tank that was based there all the time. We had greeted one another almost daily and he always had a smile for me, even in the worst of weather. I enquired if I could take a photo of him and the tank as it was my last day, and at this stage I felt that we knew one another well. He smiled as usual but shook his head. 'Not possible my friend. Security, you know.'

Unfortunately, I did know, so I shook hands with him and wished him a safe stay in Sarajevo. I could see that I was going to miss this camaraderie but I was looking forward to getting home.

HOMEWARD BOUND

I was out at the airport by lunchtime next day, along with several other people who were leaving. It was cold and misty and there were a lot of military vehicles around, the usual set-up for Sarajevo. It seemed like there were signs and tape indicating land mines everywhere. I had found the experience interesting and, if I was to be honest, quite exciting, but I needed a lot more training if I was to do more work in similar circumstances. I felt that I had not performed as well as I had expected and was making lists in my head of what I needed to do to improve. I boarded the plane with mixed emotions. The plane lifted away from the runway and I looked down on the Wounded City as we headed for home. It had been an experience!

AFTERMATH

Liz met me at Dublin airport, and I could see that she was very happy that I was back. She kept hugging me. I was glad to be home but felt confused and angry. All around me people were happy to be home for Christmas, while all I could think of were the conditions in Sarajevo. I felt terribly angry that no one seemed to care about what had happened or was happening in Bosnia. Liz said that the Christmas lights were nice at the airport and my reply was that I didn't give a damn about the lights. What was wrong with me, I wondered?

The truth, of course, was that my head had not caught up with my body. My body was in Dublin, but my head was in Sarajevo. I felt lost and terribly down. I did not know it at the time, but I was suffering from reverse culture shock, which is quite common among returning aid workers. Many find it easier to adjust to serious situations in a new setting than to adjust back to normal home life, because what they have experienced overseas in the 'new normal' for them.

GOOD ADVICE

I started to put my training plans into operation, ordered a computer and put my name down for typing and computer classes. I was determined to start filling the gaps in my education. There was a lot to be done.

One morning on my way to classes I was walking up along the Dublin quays towards O'Connell Bridge when suddenly I found myself jumping back involuntarily from an excavation in the ground. Black and yellow striped tape had been fixed around the excavation and was fluttering in the breeze. The tape was the same colour as the landmine tape and, for a second or two, I felt that I was back in Sarajevo. Some people looked at me as if I was crazy and I felt a little sheepish. At night I was having trouble sleeping and was dreaming quite a lot when I did get to sleep. When I tried to talk to Liz about it, my catchphrase was, 'You don't know what it's like, and you weren't there.' I didn't know it at the time, but Liz set about sorting me out.

A friend of mine, Jimmy, who had been overseas with the army, called to see me and asked me to go for a walk. Liz had asked him to call, but I wasn't aware of that. He told me that he knew what I was going through and offered me some advice. I doubted him until he started to list all that was going on in my head – I was glad to be home and safe and feeling guilty about feeling like that, angry that no one appeared to care about what it was like for the survivors and feeling helpless because not enough had been achieved. Jimmy explained that this was all normal and that what was happening was quite natural. He told me to take life a day at a time and that I would gradually start to feel better.

'You will be OK in a month or so,' he said, 'In the meantime try to get the most out of each day'.

I followed his advice and sure enough each day brought improvement. I did adjust but, in all honesty, an experience like that never leaves you entirely. Every so often memories of it can creep up on you when you are least expecting it. It may be hearing a song like 'Miss Sarajevo', or just the sound of Venetian blinds rattling in the wind that brings it all back.

3

Training and New Opportunities

For me 1998 was the year when it all began to come together. I started off by getting to grips with the new computer. It was not easy for me to start learning all over again and there were days when I thought that I would never understand it, but giving up was not an option.

I approached APSO again and enquired about courses involving security, communication and related topics. I was directed to Red R, which is the acronym for Registered Engineers for Disaster Relief. Red R ran courses for aid workers, and these covered a wide range of issues. I selected a course that covered communications and security – it included the use of radios and satellite phones, as well as how to deal with a wide variety of security issues. Sat-phones were a fairly new technology at that time and were bulky items that had to be set up very carefully to function properly. Setting up communication radios was again a procedure that required specific training. The actual procedures for using the equipment and recording the information (radio logs), were all done in a standardised way. I soon became completely familiar with the term 'standard operating procedure', or SOP. The security element was also something that I was very keen to learn about, particularly after my time in Bosnia.

CHILWELL BARRACKS, NOTTINGHAM

I applied for the course and had to jump through various hoops to get selected. The main problem for me was that, although the course was run by Red R in conjunction with Cable and Wireless, who looked after communications, the security end was handled by the British Army and all of the course was on an army base in the UK. To get on to the base I had to get security clearance, and this involved a lot of check-ups, as I was resident in the Republic of Ireland. After some time, clearance came through and I took the ferry to Holyhead and then drove to Nottingham, where I presented my pass and was admitted to Chilwell Barracks. I was about to meet up with the Royal Engineers again.

The course was very intense, with instruction and testing going on from early morning until late at night. We were told that scenarios would involve people wandering into minefields with detonators exploding nearby. There would be different types of gunfire, where we had to identify the weapons in use. Other scenarios would involve roadblocks, drunken soldiers and hijackings, not to mention being caught in crossfire, as well as hostage-taking. All the above was going to be thrown at us, as well as maybe a few surprises, too. I was in my element and took to the training like a duck to water.

Defused land mines were buried in the ground and live detonators were buried close by in the mock-up minefield. The detonators were set off by an electrical charge to simulate a mine explosion. Although harmless, the detonators made people jump when they were set off and certainly made us focus on the job in hand. The training was intended not only to make us aware of the dangers involved, but also to teach us how to extricate ourselves from a given situation. Getting out of a minefield intact requires a lot of patience as well as skill. It was fascinating to see how people reacted in different ways. Some freaked when the explosions took place, while others remained cool and worked patiently to get away from the danger.

I found that my sense of awareness was really heightened and that, unlike in Bosnia, I was totally focused – or so I thought.

TEAM ALPHA

The group was split into three teams, namely Alpha, Bravo, and Charlie. The initial plan was that Team Alpha would be in the Communications (Comms) Centre and would direct Team Bravo and Team Charlie, which would be getting into various problems out on the large base. I was now at ease with the phonetic alphabet! The roles would rotate so that all teams had to deal with similar problems. Teams Bravo and Charlie would report in by radio and Team Alpha would record the messages properly and relay instructions. There would also be lots of gunfire, while monitors watched to see how people dealt with the various situations that were thrown at them. It seemed to me that the best place to be for the first exercise was in the Comms Centre, and when we were asked if anyone had used a radio before, I held up my hand. Big mistake!

'OK Ray, you can lead Team Alpha,' I was told by the officer in charge.

It all seemed so simple – stay in the safety of the Comms Room and learn from the other teams' mistakes. We were quite amused at the shouting coming down the radios as the gunfire rattled. One team leader screamed about being in a minefield, while another radioed in that they were at a roadblock and were being dragged out of their vehicle. We duly recorded all reports and offered advice, as this was part of our brief. One of our team smiled as he was saying that he was glad that we were indoors and away from all the hassle when, unexpectedly, the door to the Comms room burst open and two stun grenades were thrown in.

The flashes were extremely bright and the noise deafening and totally disorientating. I found myself on the floor with an army boot in the middle of my back. I had no idea how I had ended up there. The masked 'bandits' screamed at us and demanded to know who we were and threatened to shoot us. My boots were roughly pulled from my feet and I was told to hand over any money I had. Even though it was only role-playing I could feel myself trembling as the whole scenario felt real, especially when guns were shoved into our sides. The assessors followed in after the bandits and noted how we reacted. Some got very excited, but most of our team followed the guidelines, which were to remain calm and cooperate with the 'bandits.'

After we were released from the Comms room and I had collected my boots, we swapped roles and it was our turn to be hijacked and later find ourselves in the minefield. It was hard going. Each set-up was assessed, and we were marked individually. The feedback was immensely helpful, as we were told what we were doing right and what areas we needed to improve on. It soon became fairly obvious as to who was best suited for war zone work and who would be much better deployed in more peaceful settings.

THE CLASSROOM

The classroom lectures I found fascinating, as a lot of the training involved using recordings of situations that had occurred in real life. Most of the videos had been given to the army by television stations who had filmed actual incidents, but the footage was considered too serious or distressing to air on TV. War correspondent Kate Adie seemed to lead a charmed life, as a lot of the scenarios featured her. The lecturer gave us some good advice based on the video evidence – 'If you see Kate Adie nearby, run like hell.' We learned from others' mistakes, whether it was an armoured personnel carrier driving through a mud slide (man-made) and setting off landmines, or booby-trapped doors or toilets. All of the lessons learned, I would benefit from later, especially the booby-trapped toilets.

It was fascinating to see the recordings of real-life incidents and even the simplest safety procedures made total sense. For example, BIFO is the rule that applies when parking in areas that are insecure: 'Back In – Front Out.' It meant that if you had to leave a location in a hurry, there was no time lost while you reversed your vehicle out of the parking spot. Learning to look out for places where snipers might be, and not making yourself a target, was another point that was driven home. We were told that putting up an antenna for a radio in an insecure area was a dangerous job, as you would be at a height and therefore the perfect target for a sniper. After a few days on the base I was starting to think like I really was in a war zone, such was our state of heightened awareness. The training was working.

THE BAR

On the last night of the course we went to the bar on the base for a few drinks and a soldier brought me a pint of beer. He was talking to me as if he knew me well, but I did not recognise him. He obviously realised my dilemma and after a short time explained that he was in fact one of the 'bandits' in the Comms room and held out his hand and apologised for roughing me up. In real life he was a really nice guy and as we chatted it turned out that he had been in Bosnia and, like me, had just returned home before Christmas. It seemed that I hadn't been the only person who had been a bit out of sorts coming home at Christmas. He told me that he had been the same, which was reassuring. I was intro-duced to some of the other soldiers who had been in Bosnia and felt very much at ease in their company. There was a sense of camaraderie that I again found reassuring. They had been there; they did know what it was like. We had a few drinks together and chatted about our experiences, even though mine were very limited at that stage.

I felt that the course had been very helpful as well as enjoyable and I was beginning to feel a lot more confident about working in a war zone. The training was meant to make you think differently, and for me it certainly worked. On my way back to Holyhead I decided to treat the journey as an exercise and try out some of what I had learned. I kept an eye out for potential snipers on the motorway and when I pulled into McDonald's for a quick snack, it was BIFO automatically! I even checked for landmines under my car after my meal. I was finding it hard to switch off my security brain mode, but felt more reassured. Maybe I could make a go of this after all.

HOME

I returned home to Dublin and continued to visit the library in APSO to read up on how to deal with various situations. I was also researching security issues on the internet, in particular details on landmines. It seemed that they had made a lasting impression. I was beginning to feel that I could do the job that I wanted so much, but what I really needed was another posting to try out all these new skills. I was still doing some part-time work in the construction industry but had decided that the day job in Ireland was coming to an end as I now knew what I wanted. I was ready to give it a go and felt that this time I would be better prepared than on my first mission.

RAPID RESPONSE REGISTER

It was an ad in a Sunday newspaper that gave me the opportunity I needed. The Department of Foreign Affairs had advertised for people to be put on a register for overseas work. It sounded a bit like the APSO register, but this was a new set-up. It was called the Rapid Response Register and the people selected would be trained by the Department of Foreign Affairs, with input from some aid organisations. It was envisaged that the trained personnel would be deployed in emergencies – man-made (war) or natural disasters. The personnel on the register had to be available to be deployed at short notice for use by an aid organisation, but the register and any additional training would be controlled by Foreign Affairs.

I filled in the application form, mentioning Bosnia and my latest training in security and communications. The interviews were held in mid-June and a few days later I was informed that I had been selected for inclusion on the register. I was over the moon. Within a few weeks I was involved in more training, this time in Dublin, and this also involved a lot of role-playing. I had thought previously that role-playing would not be interesting, but instead found that it was exactly what I needed. I entered each scenario as if lives depended on making the right decisions.

CONCERN WORLDWIDE

It was during this training that I met Mike Lee from Cork. We hit it off straight away and I loved his wicked sense of humour. If ever a person existed that I wanted to work with, he was that person. We seemed to complement one another. What I was weak on, he was strong in and vice versa. We seemed to be learning from one another.

On the third day of training I was called in to the office and asked to get in touch with Concern Worldwide as they wanted to discuss a possible posting with me. This I duly did, and that evening went to Concern's office for a meeting with the HR officer. The job offer was made – a logistics job for the South Sudan emergency. This would involve sourcing supplies in Kenya and making sure that the goods got into Sudan. It involved being based in Kenya, with frequent travel into the affected areas. A state of civil war existed in South Sudan and so there would be security issues. BIFO certainly wasn't a waste of time after all. I sat there in Concern's office almost in a state of shock. The situation was moving much faster than I had thought possible. I had spent years waiting for this opportunity and it was all on offer. It was now the month of July and they were talking about sending me off as soon as possible once the training was completed and my medical taken care of. I was given 24 hours to consider, although I wanted to shout 'Yes, yes, yes!' there and then.

I went home and discussed the offer with Liz first and then the family. Liz's reaction was as expected. She was fully supportive, as were the family. They wanted to know when I would be leaving and lots of details. Jenny set about making cassettes of different music for me to bring with me, the first track on the first cassette being a song by U2 called 'Bad', which is one of my favourite songs. It would remind me of home every time I played it. I was going to be away during my two sons' birthdays, which were on the same day, 16 November. Sam would be 21 and David 15. This was the second time that I was going to be away for their birthdays and I felt bad, but when I mentioned it the lads were very good about it. I was very aware of how lucky I was to have the support of my wife and three children. The families of aid workers make a lot of sacrifices. Sam laughed and asked if he could inherit my motorbike if I got blown up. I liked that, as it lightened up the atmosphere a wee bit. I told him he could.

The time went by very quickly as arrangements were made for medical check-ups and inoculations and yet more training, this time in the Concern logistics systems. Concern pointed out to me that the work involved would require two people and that I would be the senior logistics person. I enquired if I could make a recommendation for the second person and suggested that they consider Mike Lee. I was barely in the door and was requesting named people, but they seemed amused by the request. It turned out that it had been noticed how well we had bonded during the various exercises and Concern had had the exact same idea. The initial plan was for us to go for three months, but this was changed fairly quickly. In August 1998, with all my medical requirements met, I was on my way to Africa with a posting up to Christmas. What I had dreamed of for so long was now coming to pass. Mike was to follow out one week later.

DEPARTURE

A few days before I was due to leave I received a telephone call from Concern, telling me that the US embassy in Nairobi had just been blown up by a massive bomb. There had been many deaths and injuries in and around the embassy, which was in downtown Nairobi. Al Qaeda was alleged to be responsible, but at that time I had barely any knowledge of them. In view of the attack, Concern wanted to give me the opportunity to postpone or cancel my trip. The call surprised me, as the purpose of a large part of my training was to enable me to work in insecure conditions, and I had by then reached the point where I wanted to get on with it – I was really fired up. I told Concern that I was happy to travel and was keen to be on my way.

'OK' they said, 'If you are sure, you leave next week.'

I left Dublin on a Monday morning and flew to London. The plan was to go to Concern's office in London, spend 3 days going over the Sudan details with an experienced logistician who had worked in Kenya and Sudan and then continue on to Nairobi on Wednesday evening. The three days in London flew by and I felt that the time there had been well spent as I absorbed yet more information. However I was missing my family already and even considered flying back home for just one night. It was only a one hour flight, but when I thought further about it I realised that as hard as it had been to leave the first time, it would be even harder to go through the whole departure scenario again and so I telephoned home before I took the tube to the airport. It was an emotional call. As I boarded the plane in Heathrow I was anxious, excited and missing my family, but determined that I was going to see the job through. There would be no turning back. The pace had been hectic in the last few weeks with hardly a minute to spare but, as it turned out, it was nothing compared to the pace I experienced once I arrived in Africa.

4

Kenya and South Sudan

NAIROBI

I arrived in Nairobi early on Thursday morning and was brought to the office while my luggage was left in the Concern apartment, which was a short distance away. I was put into the care of Richard from Dublin, a young man of boundless energy, who it seemed could turn his hand to anything and everything. I was introduced to the staff, had photographs taken for security passes, was given a quick rundown on the radio system and had briefings from several people. Hitting the ground running was the order of the day.

The rebel army in the south of Sudan, the Sudan People's Liberation Army (SPLA) and the government forces in the north were at war, which was having a terrible effect on the civilian population there. Small farmers and their families had been driven off their land and were starving to death. With increasing malnutrition, the very young and very old were the first to suffer, resulting in serious medical problems. The SPLA had a political wing called the Sudanese People's Liberation Movement (SPLM). A travel pass was necessary to go into South Sudan and this was issued by the SPLM. By Thursday afternoon I had my pass. There was no hanging about here, I could see.

Richard told me that I was to travel the following day, Friday, to the town of Lokichoggio, or Loki, as it was known. Loki was right on the border and was the main distribution point for all aid going into Sudan. It was nearly two hours' flying time from Nairobi and I would be spending a few days there, getting briefed on what was immediately required in the various Concern working areas in Sudan. As the emergency operation had only been up and running quite a short time, there was a lot to be done. On Friday morning I left Nairobi in the company of the Concern country director (CD). We flew to Loki on a 12-seater plane and I really enjoyed the experience. The temperature in Nairobi had been a comfortable 25 degrees centigrade, but when I stepped out of the plane in Loki it was like stepping into an oven. The temperature there was normally 47 degrees during the day.

LOKI

Loki was a very strange place, I heard many people say, but probably more correctly, it had been taken over by people who became stranger day by day. It is situated in the north-east of Kenya and, for good measure, was in disputed territory between Kenya and Sudan. Our compound had been constructed by another NGO, Norwegian People's Aid (NPA) and it was here that we had our office and accommodation.

The basic accommodation consisted of tents, while the upmarket version consisted of timber huts with grass roofs. The timber was very rough and irregular in shape and when used to build the outside walls, there were often big gaps in between the planks. This was a bit of a problem, as there were many snakes around, so there was plastic sheeting lining the inside of the walls – a simple solution to a dangerous problem. There were individual huts that slept two, and a terrace of huts called Madd House terrace. The inside of the huts was like an oven, but we gradually adjusted to the extremes in temperature. Several other NGOs were also living and working in the NPA compound so there was a lot of banter going on all the time. It reminded me of the TV series M*A*S*H. In the middle was a canteen and meeting place, a circular building with a grass roof. There were shower cubicles around the compound. Water was poured into several 40-gallon drums that were on timber supports. The drums had been painted matte black so the sun warmed them up during the day and we could have warm showers in the evening. The toilets consisted of pits dug in the ground and had black plastic screens around them to give privacy. They were known as VIP latrines, which stood for 'ventilated improved pit' latrines. They were an improved version of the standard latrine, which was not ventilated. We were grateful for small mercies! We had an armed guard at night who carried an AK-47 assault rifle. Home sweet home.

The local tribe were the Turkana, a tall and graceful people who were basically small farmers. They were a very private sort of people, living quietly in the middle of the bush, when it was decided by the powers that be that Loki would be a good place to build an airstrip. It was conveniently located nearly two hours' flying time from Nairobi and right on the border with Sudan. One minute there were goats and camels grazing in the bush and next there were hundreds of international aid workers, not to mention lots of planes of different sizes, from massive C-130 Hercules cargo planes used by the UN for airdrops, down to little Cessnas and Antonovs.

From Friday to Monday I had meetings in Loki, mainly with the nutritionists who advised me on what they needed – and they emphasised that everything was needed urgently. The details of the numbers and location of the various beneficiaries were passed on to me, with the ration allowances etc. The basic information was provided by the teams, but it was up to logistics (or logs, as we were called) to work out the finer details. In spite of the training that I had received before going out, it was all a bit daunting, but the urgency of the situation registered quickly. Schedules and time frames were drawn up and lots of discussions held as to how we could meet the demands for supplies. There were different teams in various locations and of course they all felt that they should have priority.

The Concern person in charge in Loki at that stage was a man called Predip, who had lots of experience and had been brought in from another country just to set up the Sudan operation. He had set up a large store and had the people in place for us to run the logistics operation. While the setting-up work in Loki had been going on, teams had gone into Sudan, carried out surveys and reached agreements with other NGOs on who should work where. Without cooperation and coordination in the early stages, there would have been total chaos. Predip had been in Loki for ten weeks, working at least fourteen hours a day, seven days a week, and he was exhausted. He provided some really helpful suggestions as to how the operation should be run overall. I was a bit in awe of all that he had arranged, but he was very modest and simply pointed out to me that it would be my responsibility and Mike's to move the operation on to the next stage.

The goods required had to be purchased in Nairobi and sent to Loki by road or air. They were then offloaded and held in storage until they were forwarded by air to the various places in Sudan. Air transport was necessary because there were no roads as such in Sudan. Everything had to be planned and accounted for, which involved local logisticians, storekeepers, trucks and, last but not least, aircraft. Predip provided all the details of how long it took to fly to the various places in Sudan and introduced me to the concept of the rotation. A rotation involved a plane being fuelled, loaded with cargo and flying to its destination, offloading, refuelling if necessary, and returning to Loki. The same procedure was followed several times throughout the day as rotation followed rotation. The UN carried out air drops using large C-130 Hercules cargo planes and their rotations were referred to as sorties. In Loki there were no landing lights and no radar, so air traffic control was basic, to say the least. The lack of these basics caused one or two problems, as we soon found out.

AIRCRAFT AND AIRSTRIPS

My learning curve about aircraft was very steep. When I analysed what had to be sent to our various bases in Sudan, I looked at what aircraft could be hired and started making plans in my head for using the bigger private planes. My logic was simple – the bigger the plane, the lower the number of rotations. I then learned that the length of the airstrip was critical and that the bigger the plane, the longer the airstrip required. The simple fact was that I had to match the aircraft required to the airstrip length that was available. I soon had details from Predip of all the planes available for hire, their carrying capacity and the length of airstrip required.

The airstrip at Loki was hard surface, built under UN supervision. As there were no landing lights, take-off and landing had to be done in natural light. The first planes rolled down the strip at exactly 0630 hours for take-off, and they had to be back on the ground at night-time by no later than 1800 hours. Dusk comes very suddenly in that part of the world and although it could be bright enough at 1750 hours, by 1800 hours it was like someone had just switched off the lights. I spent many an anxious time up at that airstrip waiting for a plane to return, only to see a light appear over the mountains in Sudan and then touch down in Loki just before darkness closed in. To me the pilots were heroes, but also a bit crazy. I liked it there. By Monday evening I was ready to leave Loki and return to Nairobi to start getting prices and commence purchasing. Our rules stated that we had to have three quotes for any purchases over 300 US dollars, so we were constantly under pressure.

EVACUATIONS AND MEDEVACS

During the initial discussions in Loki it was pointed out to me by some of the teams that, as it was still very early in the programme, no contracts had been formally agreed for evacuations and medevacs. Evacuation was the general term given for extracting people out of an area in a hurry, due to security considerations. Medevacs amounted to the same thing, except that the consideration in that case was medical. I was introduced to one of the owners of the charter company 748 Air Services at the Loki airstrip on the Monday evening. We were flying back to Nairobi on his company's aircraft and this presented a good opportunity for me to discuss evacuations and medevacs. By the time we had landed in Nairobi we had reached an agreement and had arranged to meet the next day to sign a contract. I found the flight back to Nairobi different from the norm, as the plane was a mixture of cargo, passengers, animals, bikes and whatnot. We sat up on top of a load of sacks and negotiated on the move. I liked the different way of doing business and really got a buzz from the speed at which business matters could be sorted out. When we landed in Nairobi I waited around at the arrivals hall in Jomo Kenyatta airport, as Mike was flying in that evening from London and I had arranged to meet him there.

MIKE'S FIRST DAYS

After I met Mike at the airport, we travelled on to the apartment that Concern had rented and I started briefing him on what I had seen so far. He was to be based in Loki, while I would be based in Nairobi, but as the job description indicated, I would frequently travel to Loki and various places in Sudan. The reference to frequent travel turned out to be absolutely true and I was to spend the next 50 days without a break and working long hours between Nairobi, Loki, and various places in Sudan.

Mike and I worked together in Nairobi for the next few days on the logistics and it was during this time that I had my first experience of Mike's knowledge of radios and all matters electrical. Mike was a qualified electrician and one of his hobbies was amateur ham radios. He had a radio operator's licence and lots of experience. While he was looking at the radio set-up he was informed that the signal could be a bit weak at times. This was a challenge that he could not resist.

'No problem,' he said. 'I can sort that out if someone can bring me to an electrical shop!'

He was driven into the city and returned a short time later with copper wire. He proceeded to put the copper wire around the radio antenna and when he was finished, the signal was a lot stronger. However, that was not the end of the story. When we were on the telephone, every so often we could hear radio messages over the phone. The NGO *Médecins Sans Frontières* (MSF) was located just down the road from us and they complained that their telephone conversations were being interrupted by our radio messages. Mike went to check it out and it turned out that the local overhead telephone wires were not insulated and were picking up the boosted radio signal, so the copper wire had to be removed. We had solved one problem but created another. However, when it came to radio problems in the field, Mike was the first to be consulted and was always able to sort out the problems.

By Thursday evening we were ready to go back to Loki together to start working on that end of the supply line. It was a bit of a shock when I realised that I had only been in Africa a week and yet we had sent out enquiries, gotten quotations back and the first batch of goods had been ordered and was on its way to Loki. I felt like I had been there a month instead of a week, such was the pace.

SNAKES

On Friday morning Mike and I flew to Loki and met up with an exhausted Predip, who was due to hand over to Mike. It was his last week in Loki and he was due to go on R&R (rest and relaxation) in Mombasa before he returned home. Predip warned us to be careful of snakes. He told us not to leave the doors of our huts open, to bang our boots off the ground in the mornings just in case there was a snake inside, and to be careful when we went into cool, dark places. A few days later, Predip was working with Mike when he left the office to go to the latrine, which was a short distance away. When he walked in he found a cobra hanging from the roof timbers. Cobras spit at their intended victims before they attack, and this cobra spat into Predip's eye. He reacted very quickly and spun back out the doorway and called for Mike. Mike realised that he had to act quickly and immediately took him up to the local makeshift hospital. A special eye wash was provided, with the instructions to wash the affected eye every half hour, which Mike did right through the night. Predip had been warned that his sight could be affected, but luckily he made a full recovery. He came to Nairobi a few days after the snake attack and was very shaken up. He decided that he would drop his plans for R&R in Mombasa and returned home. It was a lesson to us all, never to drop your guard where snakes are concerned.

Mike moved into Predip's hut in Loki and settled in quickly. I was with him one evening in the compound when there was a huge commotion with shouts of, 'Snake, snake!' One had been seen going into a gap in the timber in the wall of Mike's hut. We got the security guard, who was armed, and peeped in the door to see if we could make out the snake. We could not see anything, but as the security guard stepped backwards he stood on a boot that had been removed from the room. He jumped around shouting and pointed his gun at the boot. There were a lot of spectators crowding around the door and offering advice, but as soon as the guard pointed the gun at the boot they all scattered. When the guard realised that it was not a snake he had stood on he relaxed and all the spectators roared laughing and someone shouted, 'Don't shoot the boot, don't shoot the boot!' We could see the funny side of all this, but there was still the matter of the snake and where it was hiding. Mike agreed to sleep in my room that night, but next morning told me that he had not slept all night due to my snoring and that he was going back to his own hut that night.

'At least the bloody snake will not be snoring!' was his comment as he went out the door.

DALE

Dale was an American I disliked the first time I met him. He was definitely not PC, but as I got to know him better I became fond of him and for some strange reason we clicked. He was in his early fifties and had been a B52 bomber pilot during the Vietnam War (or maybe more correctly, some said, during the American war in Vietnam). He made no apologies for his time in Vietnam and could make quite provocative statements at times. He had what could be called a fireman's sense of humour and there was something about him that made people wonder what exactly he was doing in a disaster zone. As I got to know him better, I realised that there was a lot more to him than the image he projected, although he really was an enigma. He was a law unto himself and this caused problems on more than one occasion, but if he decided that you were OK, he would literally go through gunfire to get you out of trouble. He seemed to have standard tests for evaluating people, which basically involved scaring the hell out of them and then seeing how they would react.

The first time that I flew with him he asked if I wanted to sit in the co-pilot's seat and when I replied that I would, he told the co-pilot to take a seat in the back, – only not in such polite terms. I wasn't aware that he was testing me and was delighted to sit up front for a while, but heard later that if you refused the invitation, he simply gave up on you at that stage. His next test was to ask you if you would like to take over flying the plane and he would sit there and instruct away as if this was an everyday occurrence. For me, the scariest time was when he came in to land. If he was in his 'scare the hell out of them' mood he approached the airstrip at a very steep angle, almost vertically it seemed, and flattened out at the very last minute for landing. Again, he would check to see how people reacted. If you laughed, he was thrilled. I enjoyed the antics and believed that he really loved flying and wasn't going to wreck the aircraft, or us – he was just having fun.

Not everyone felt the same way though. There was the camp that said Dale was the greatest pilot ever, while there were many more who felt that he was dangerous. I belonged to the former, but Mike was very definitely of the latter. He refused point blank to fly with Dale and whenever possible, avoided using small planes at all. This suited me fine, as I could fly when it was necessary, and Mike could stay on the ground. We were both doing what we liked best. Dale loved the excitement of emergency work and it seemed that he just could not settle into a routine existence. He told me that he had been married three times and –the clincher – each time to a schoolteacher. 'I just don't seem to be able to resist the schoolteachers,' he would say. He told me

Mr Ray Would Like a Monkey

that he had an oil well in Texas, where he came from, and that he was a millionaire, but that he got bored when he was back in the US, while he was never bored when working in Africa. I was never sure what to believe, but he seemed genuine enough. He was the man to solve problems, although he was not averse to creating a few as well.

WHAT'S YOUR NAME?

As part of the security set-up, every new person coming to work in Kenya and Sudan was given a code name and all the locations we worked in were also referred to by code. This was to ensure that people listening in on the radio traffic could not identify who was going where, although some of the codes for places seemed fairly obvious. Using people's real names on the radio was forbidden and so most of us did not know the real names of a lot of our colleagues. At first this seemed strange, but after a while general conversation was conducted more in radio speak that normal English. New people coming into the team found this very odd at first, but quickly adapted and within a short time would be communicating with each other in radio speak and code as if they had always been doing it.

The first job in the morning, wherever you were in Sudan, was to check in by radio to Loki and give an update on the security situation, in code, and then a weather report. The weather report was to facilitate the delivery of supplies by air and consisted of a choice of three conditions: dry and landable, wet and landable or unlandable. The weather in Sudan could be unpredictable, as some places were suffering from drought and other areas were experiencing flooding. The weather and security report were especially important, because in many cases planes would have been loaded the night before for transporting goods to Sudan. As the planes started to queue up before 0630 hours for departure, it was essential to know as early as possible if the planes could land at their destination. For this reason, the first radio call went out at 0530 hours from Loki, to confirm that all was OK at the destination

The difficulty, if you were in Sudan, was that there was a one-hour time difference between Kenya and Sudan, so the person giving the report from Sudan had to be on the radio at 0430 hours. If the report was that the plane could not land, then the goods were unloaded from the plane as quickly as possible and the goods for the second rotation loaded. The second rotation might not have been allocated to us, and so there were a lot of negotiations with other agencies when this sort of situation arose. The radio report was therefore a very important part of the logistical operation. Once you lost your spot in the queue for rotations, it was gone, and you went to the back of the queue that day or had to wait for another day. 'Dry and landable,' was music to our ears, especially for the first rotation. The one exception to this strict adherence to the rotation plan was when a medevac or evacuation was required. When that happened, agreement was reached either to change the plans or to divert an aircraft so that a person could be extracted out of Sudan as quickly as possible. 'Medevac required,' was not what you wanted to hear.

TONGE

I had been in Kenya for only a couple of weeks when I was informed that it would be a good idea to see a camp that was up and running in Sudan. It was in a place called Tonge, not too far from Loki. The camp was for internally displaced people and referred to as an IDP camp. Refugee camps are for people who are displaced but have crossed a border to escape from a situation, but as all our beneficiaries were Sudanese, they were classified as IDPs. I was still learning at this stage and booked a flight from Loki to Tonge. I was a bit concerned about how I would react at seeing people in a distressed state, as I had found it quite upsetting in Sarajevo. I was accompanied by the head nutritionist from Concern, who explained the various steps to assess people for malnutrition. Although the assessment is carried out in a detailed, scientific way, it is straightforward enough and I could understand the procedures involved. This involved measuring children's height and then checking what they should weigh

Mr Ray Would Like a Monkey

against a height chart supplied by the World Health Organisation (WHO). The theoretical weight was then recorded. The children were then weighed, and their actual weight expressed as a percentage of the theoretical weight. The percentage reading was then used as a basis for deciding what action, if any, was to be taken. The procedure was known as weight-to-height measurement. They also used a special measuring tape to measure the mid-upper arm circumference (MUAC) of a child and the information from this procedure was used to ascertain the child's status. Another indicator was the colour of the children's hair, which, of course, should have been black. If it had turned orange, I was told, then we needed to investigate further. I was still learning and had lots more to absorb. The nutritionists were highly organised when it came to collecting data and entering children into the programme for treatment.

The camp in Tonge was quite large and to my surprise had been split into three sections. The first and largest was for women and children, with a small number of old men. Food called Unimix, which is a porridge-like food with added vitamins, was being prepared in large pots over wood fires. I was immediately struck by the smell of hundreds of people crowded into a fairly limited space. The second part of the camp consisted mostly of old, blind people. The blind were helped by younger children, who acted as their guides. The third part housed people with leprosy. I questioned this division, as it added a lot of work for those trying to organise the supplying of food and was told that it was not acceptable culturally for any of these groups to mix. Another lesson learned.

I managed to have some conversations, through our interpreter, with people from each group. It was my first experience of meeting people who suffered from leprosy. The locals were terrified of catching the disease, although it is a bloodborne disease and cannot be passed on by touch. The smiles and welcome from the people with leprosy, many of whom were missing part of their hands, made me feel quite humble and I wondered how I would cope if I had their problems. As if this wasn't enough, they now had to contend with the ongoing war.

Our visit also caused a lot of excitement with the children. The camp managers tried to keep life as normal as possible for them, in that they held school under a tree. It was breaktime and the children were queuing up with plastic plates for their food. I noticed one little girl who had a badly injured hand and enquired what had happened to her. She was very hungry, I was told, and had tried to steal some food. She was caught and her mother punished her by putting her hand into boiling water. I was shocked and asked how a mother could do such a thing to her own child. It seemed that this was expected, as otherwise someone else would have done it to punish her. You have to learn not to interfere in their culture, I was informed. Obviously, I still had a lot more to learn about how to deal with different situations.

While the children were collecting their food one little boy came and stood beside us. He was about five years old. He kept smiling at us and I enquired about him through our guide. The boy had been from a family of six and was the sole survivor. For some reason he seemed to stand out from all the other children, and I commented on this.

'He's the one with the 401 factor,' she said.

I was not familiar with the expression until she explained.

'You can be dealing with four hundred of them and remain detached, but sometimes one will catch your eye and that is the one that gets to you. We call it the 401 factor.' It wasn't too long before I understood exactly what she meant.

We made our way back to the landing strip and the pilot angrily asked what had kept us. We had agreed to depart at 1200 hours, and he was complaining that we were nearly an hour late. We disagreed, advising that it wasn't quite 1200 hours yet.

'It might be 1200 hours here,' he said, 'but it is 1300 hours in Kenya and all arrival and departure times are based on Kenya time.'

Mr Ray Would Like a Monkey

We had been going by local time, thinking that this was the correct procedure. I realised what a problem time differences could be in the future if we were not very careful. Shortly afterwards, the time difference was the underlying factor in a serious situation when a film crew from the BBC was nearly fired on as their plane approached another location in South Sudan. Soon we were on our way out of Tonge, heading back to Loki. Even now, after all these years, I still have trouble getting my head around the idea of deliberately scalding your own child. And the smell in an IDP camp is something that you never forget!

SUPPLIES REQUESTS

The pace was relentless and the radio seemed to be chattering nonstop with requests for supplies of all types. All supplies had to be requested and authorised on a document called a Supplies Request. This had to be approved and coded so that the finance department could allocate the costs involved against the various programmes. It was an emergency, for sure, but shortcuts in the paperwork could not be allowed. We had a large store in Loki that was basically a very large rubber tent, called a rub hall. It had a storage capacity of 1000 cubic metres. Goods that we required on an ongoing basis, including rice, water treatment tablets, stationery, pens, tents etc. were stored in Loki. There was one storekeeper and two assistants. The rules indicated that the goods could be obtained or released only when an authorised supply request was produced. The requests came in from Sudan to Loki and anything that could be supplied from Loki was sent back as quickly as possible. Goods that were not available from the Loki store had to be purchased in Nairobi or further afield and then sent by plane or road to Loki. With a staff of different nationalities it was easy to have misunderstandings about what was actually required. 'Lost in translation,' was a term used often. Even Australian English, American English and Irish English sometimes seemed like vastly different languages.

There was also the matter that people requesting special goods or tools sometimes did not consider how the goods could be delivered. We had a request for a ten-foot-long drill bit for a hand auger that was to be used to drill for water. The concept was fine, except that we could not get a ten-foot-long drill bit into a small plane! Each supply request form had an ID number in the top right-hand corner and then twelve separate lines, with each line numbered. This allowed for varying quantities of twelve different types of items to be requested on any one sheet. At one stage we had at least 30 supply request forms being processed, which meant that we had to purchase 360 items in varying quantities (30 sheets x 12 items per sheet) and deliver them to Loki for forwarding on to various places in Sudan. The organising of the supplies and following up on them took some doing, although we had some simple systems that involved a file for each location, and all enquiries to us about outstanding requests had to have the supply request (SR) number and line number indicated. Only in this way could we quickly identify any item in question. We also had blank SR's beside the radio and when the details were radioed in, we filled in the blank forms. Then when the originals arrived, these were stapled to the 'radio copy', as it was known. It was necessary to have these simple systems as, without a SOP, chaos would quickly ensue.

YEI

We had an office close to the Red Cross hospital in a town called Yei in Sudan. Rumour had it that the Red Cross flags were being used as direction finders for planes on bombing missions. Red Cross hospitals had been bombed several times from the air and our team in Yei were noted for their calm approach to such happenings. We had also been informed that anti-personnel landmines had been laid in the area. The team radioed in one afternoon to inform me in code that they were under bombardment again. The radio report was all very calm and there was no indication of any stress at all. 'We have some seagulls visiting and leaving eggs in our location,' was the message. Evacuation was not requested, but I was asked to send on some details on how to build a bomb shelter. My lessons learned with Red R and the

Royal Engineers were being put to use. The bomb shelter was duly constructed by digging a five-foot-deep hole in the ground and then placing timber over the hole at ground level. The excavated soil was then placed over the timber to form a roof and some steps were cut out in the ground leading down to the shelter. Everyone, it seemed, was pleased with the new Mark 1 bomb shelter. When the bombers came again the team headed for the shelter – only for the first people down the steps to back out again very quickly. It was shady in the bomb shelter, obviously enough, and the local snakes had decided that this was the best place to escape the searing heat. Bomb-proof shelters, maybe, but certainly not snake-proof.

On another afternoon we had a radio call from Yei requesting supplies. I was filling in the radio version of the supply request and was surprised to find a new tyre for a Toyota Land Cruiser on the list. As the cars we were using were fairly new, I enquired why they needed a new tyre. They informed me that they had been on a dirt track road when they met a truck coming from the opposite direction. They had to drive onto the edge of the track to avoid the truck, where unfortunately the tyre was blown off by a landmine. There were no injuries to the staff and they sent their apologies for wrecking the tyre! Their calm and laidback approach certainly had a calming effect on me, but there were times when I wondered what the next radio call would bring. I had been told in training that you must be calm and generate confidence when dealing with serious situations over the radio. Well, the team in Yei certainly worked to that guideline.

WONDER WOMAN

News was spreading that there had been another aerial bombardment in Yei. A local woman had been injured by shrapnel just outside the hospital and had been carried in for treatment. She was bleeding from the shoulder, but then complained about an injury to her thigh – a small bomblet from the cluster bomb was buried in the soft tissue of her thigh. This caused some panic, as the bomblet had not exploded, but that did not mean that it would remain stable. The woman was placed on a table and told not to move. A surgeon advised that he knew nothing about bombs and that what was needed was a de-miner or ordnance expert. One was located and brought quickly to the hospital. The surgeon and de-miner worked together. The de-miner removed the unexploded device and the surgeon then dealt with her injuries. This amazing occurrence became the talk of Loki and raised the question – who was the hero of the hour?

After much discussion is was agreed that the de-miner was doing his job, the surgeon was doing his job and the patient was the hero because, if she had panicked, all three could have perished. The woman was evacuated out to Loki hospital and given further treatment there. I saw her shortly afterwards with her arm in a sling, limping around the hospital grounds, and felt that I was truly in the presence of an amazing person. Someone said that a real hero is the coward who doesn't run away. Well, this woman had remained calm under the most extraordinary circumstances. Ordinary people can show such courage when least expected.

NYAMLEL

Another team was working in a place called Nyamlel. They were distributing food in the area and had extended their distribution to another location called Marial Bai. The two places were connected by river, but the team were travelling overland, which was very time-consuming. A boat that had belonged to UNICEF was located in Nyamlel and we were informed that we could borrow it. It was quite a large boat and because of the flow in the river we needed an engine, as it would have been impossible to row against the current. A supply request came in for a 15 HP outboard engine. We searched Nairobi but there is no call for outboard engines there. Eventually we had to arrange for the engine to be purchased in Mombasa and sent up to Nairobi. It was flown to Loki and then sent on to Nyamlel. Mike went to Nyamlel to train our local staff in how to set up and run the engine, as well as how to service it. It had taken a lot of effort to get the engine to its final destination, but now the transport time for getting food to Marial Bai had been cut from several days to just a few hours. It also meant that if an evacuation was required, we could get out of Nyamlel not just by plane, but also by boat.

VICTOR OSCAR

At one point we required cement for several different projects in Sudan and it was coming by road from Nairobi to Loki. We were short three or four bags and had a rotation booked for the next morning, so we were keen to get some as soon as possible. I headed up to another compound to see what I could scrounge. I asked the logistician for a loan of four bags, but he referred me to the manager, Victor Oscar. I assured him that we could replace it in a few days, but he was reluctant, as he had been told that story by other people and he was still waiting. I could understand his position and was about leave when I noticed a calendar beside his desk. The calendar had pictures of BMW motorbikes on it. I enquired if he was interested in motorbikes and he produced photographs of his own bike. I told him that I had a Honda back in Ireland and he invited me to sit down and we had a chat about different bikes. A short while later I got up to go, having enjoyed the chat. Just as I was about to leave he asked me how many bags of cement I needed and the deal was done.

I never did find out what Victor Oscar's real name was. I enquired later around Loki and was told that his father was also working in Loki and that his name was Golf Oscar, but that was as much as I could find out about his name. Security procedures were working well when we did not know who we were actually getting cement from.

MEDEVAC

We continued to be extremely busy in Concern Nairobi and the team were working very hard to keep up with all the demands on our time. One morning an email was circulated informing the staff that the Nairobi office now had responsibility for procurement for the emergency in nearby Somalia. However, on checking this out, I was told that most of the goods required in Somalia were purchased locally in Mogadishu and apart from the odd trip there to give technical support, there would be little increase in my workload. I made several arrangements to visit our office in Mogadishu, but just as I was due to travel, the trip was cancelled for security reasons. It seemed that it was nearly impossible to approach or land at the main airport in Mogadishu. This situation continued for several weeks and I was so busy between Nairobi and Loki that Somalia was not on my mind much.

One day in October, however, I was on the radio to Loki from Nairobi and had just finished receiving details of yet more goods required when a garbled radio call came in. All I could hear was 'Charlie November, Charlie November,' which was our call sign in Nairobi, and then static. I requested the caller to repeat their message and automatically went into radio speak.

'Station calling Charlie November, we have a bad copy, send again.'

This meant that I could not make out the message and was requesting them to transmit again.

They kept calling us, but it was a few minutes before I could make out anything at all. I called Richard into the radio room and asked him if he could make out the message. We identified the word 'emergency' among the static but were still having problems understanding everything else. Eventually we heard the words 'Charlie Mike' and we looked at each other as it dawned on us that this was the office from Mogadishu calling us.

It took a while to decipher the message, but the gist of it was that their senior man in charge was terribly ill and they needed a medical evacuation as soon as possible. I made an announcement over the radio telling everyone to stand by, that as we were dealing with an emergency, they would have to wait. This is normal procedure. Unless you are involved directly in the emergency, you stay quiet and listen. I was later told that there were lots of listeners that day! Medevac requests are treated in the same way as a mayday call, where very specific information is relayed in all situations. The SOP when sending a mayday is to advise: who you are, where you are, the nature of the problem and assistance required, the number of people involved and any other relevant information.

It is the duty of the radio operator receiving the call to take charge of the situation and to remain calm at all times. This can be an incredibly stressful job but is hugely satisfying when all goes well. For this medevac we needed the name of the patient, where he could be collected from, what the medical problem was, how many people would be travelling and their names, and anything else that could help. We were informed that just the patient would be travelling and that he could be picked up from a particular airport near Mogadishu. With all the static on the radio it was very difficult to get all the information, but we eventually had the minimum info required and set about making contact with the aircraft people who would do the pick-up. The immediate problem was that all the agreements we had in place for medevacs were for getting people out of Sudan and, as we had just taken over support for Somalia, this was new territory for us. Nonetheless, we very quickly made contact with one company that had a plane that had just left for Loki with goods on board. It was agreed that the plane would return to Nairobi, unload the cargo, refuel and file a flight plan to Mogadishu. We were now getting regular radio updates from Charlie Mike (Mogadishu) and the news was not good. Due to a lot of fighting and gunfire in Mogadishu they could not make progress to the airport. The airport itself was now also being subjected to gunfire. We had a problem.

The aircraft company suggested a solution. We were to ask the people in Somalia if they could make their way to another airstrip called K50, 50 kilometres from central Mogadishu. That might seem quite a short distance, but in a country with a civil war raging, it is a considerable distance and not for the faint-hearted. They advised their ETA at K50, which was relayed by us to the aircraft company. This was going to require careful timing. The aircraft would land and stay on the ground just long enough to load the patient and would then take off immediately. The team in Somalia headed for K50, informed us regularly by radio of their location and I relayed that information by telephone to the aircraft company in Nairobi. The aircraft company then sent the information on the aircraft frequency to the pilot and in this way the plan was coordinated. When the aircraft company were satisfied that the team were getting near the landing strip, they authorised the plane to fly in. Sometime later I received a message by radio confirming that the patient had been handed over and the words, 'Thank you Charlie November'. I breathed a sigh of relief. This was no time to get sentimental, but I felt a lump in my throat. So far, so good.

The aircraft company telephoned me later and gave me the ETA for the aircraft into Nairobi, so I headed out to Wilson airport to collect him. The patient was a man called Alpha Romeo, and when I saw him being helped off the plane I was quite worried. He looked so frail. I got him into our car and we headed off to the nearby hospital, where we had an arrangement for all Concern staff to be treated. The arrangement was that we updated our staff list every time a new person arrived in the country and the hospital had a memorandum of understanding (MOU), whereby we agreed to pay all medical costs involved. Your name had to be on the approved list, otherwise you would not be admitted unless you paid a lot of money upfront. The patient was seen by a doctor and after some time the doctor returned and informed me that the patient had a stomach ulcer that was bleeding and that he also had malaria. He was extremely ill. I asked for him to be admitted, but as his name was not on the staff list, the hospital refused. He was given medication and told to come back in the morning. I brought him to our apartment, but a short time later he looked worse, so I got a driver to bring us back to the hospital. This time I approached the desk, explained that the man with me had just arrived in the country, would be on the updated staff list in the morning and that I wanted him admitted. There was a bit of a heated discussion, but eventually they relented and admitted him. It was nearly midnight at this stage and I felt exhausted.

Once he was in hospital I could relax. Up to that point I had been running on adrenaline. Alpha Romeo made a good recovery and I was shocked to see a few days later that he was quite a young man. He came to our apartment to recuperate and we got to know each other well. I was pleased at the outcome and felt that our medevacs were working, although the stress of overseeing these procedures and giving the impression of being totally calm was not easy to deal with, to say the least. He said that he owed me a big favour and that he would not forget what had been done for him.

Years later, in 2008, I was working for the UN in Nairobi overseeing the transport of supplies into Somalia. We were trying to enter into a partnership arrangement with an NGO whereby various items could be distributed on our behalf to IDPs in Mogadishu. This is a common arrangement, where the UN provides supplies to various NGOs and the NGOs arrange the distribution of the UN supplies alongside their own distribution. I was told by some of my UN colleagues that it was very difficult to get goods distributed in Somalia, especially in Mogadishu, due to the security situation. I said that I would see what could be done and after some enquiries found that Alpha Romeo was back in Mogadishu and still working for Concern. I got in touch with him and asked him if he remembered me. He came to Nairobi a few days later and an arrangement was made for Concern to support the UN operation in Mogadishu. He had returned the favour.

AJIEP

We were up to our eyes in requests for supplies when a meeting was called in the office in Nairobi. MSF were running a programme in a place in Sudan called Ajiep and the situation there was very serious. The town had been attacked and the local population had fled and hidden in the swamps nearby. We were informed that Concern would be going to work in Ajiep alongside MSF, as the situation required additional resources. I was a bit dismayed at this news, as we were already stretched to the limit, so I requested additional logistics staff. Without more staff we were going to slow down the existing work. It seemed that we were flat out and now we had to up the pace again. This often happens in emergency work, as it is nearly impossible to say no, but at the same time we needed to be realistic about what we could achieve.

The plan was to send in a survey team of nutritionists, nurses and a doctor to Ajiep to establish what our level of activity would be. Some initial planning was carried out and supplies requests were prepared, listing all that might be needed. The details would be finalised after the initial assessment. We had everyday items like tents and some tinned foods etc. in stock, which would be made available to the assessment team. I was asked to travel with the team so that the logistics needs could be determined first-hand. I went to Loki in preparation for the trip, but each day the radio report from MSF stated that the airstrip was wet and unlandable. After three days I had lots of work backing up in Nairobi and had to make the decision to return there. Every minute was precious now.

The day after I returned to Nairobi the assessment team got the green light to fly in to Ajiep. The airstrip was beside a river and this was to prove a problem. The team were doing their assessment when the level of the river started to rise rapidly. There had been flooding upriver and a lot of water was now flowing towards Ajiep. There was a sharp bend on the river and within a very short time the river had flooded onto the surrounding land and washed away a lot of the supplies the team had brought in with them. Unfortunately the airstrip was one of the first places flooded. The team had been carrying a portable short-wave radio called a Q-Mac, which was fixed in a rucksack-like harness and used for sending back information. The message came in that the team had lost most of their supplies in the flash flood. MSF were able to offer some assistance, but basically all that the team had was what they were wearing. They needed help as quickly as possible but, with the airstrip flooded, it was impossible to fly in.

Meetings were held and proposals made as to how to solve the problem. We had the details of what they needed and

Mr Ray Would Like a Monkey

the supplies were quickly put together. The big question was transport. Several solutions were discussed, including landing somewhere else and sending the supplies overland, but that was discounted for a number of reasons. It seemed that Ajiep was cut off by land and by air. The feasibility of going further upriver and sending the supplies downriver by boat were examined but, due to security and the flooding river, this was not an option at the time. The use of helicopter supply and even hovercraft was raised, but as we did not have either at this stage, we were clutching at straws. A few days had now passed and the situation had not improved at the airstrip. The word was that it could be weeks before the strip would be dry enough to land on. We had a crisis meeting in Nairobi and the message was that it was a logistics problem and that we were to sort it. I was a bit peeved at this attitude and it made me all the more determined to try and find a solution.

We considered dropping supplies by parachute but were told that this was not feasible with the aircraft that were available to us. Eventually Mike and I approached Dale and asked if he had a plane that could do an air drop. He considered this and when I saw a grin spreading across his face, I thought that maybe we had it cracked. First he wanted to know the details. We explained what had happened and his reply was typical Dale. He wanted to know who was stranded. I told him and he commented that he did not like doctors, as one had told him previously that an airstrip was landable and it had turned out not to be. As a result, the front wheel of the plane had buried itself in the soft soil. As if this hadn't been bad enough, when he complained to the doctor involved, the doctor had told him to put the plane into reverse to get it out. Dale had decided after that occasion that he was not going to cooperate with doctors anymore – as well as avoiding schoolteachers! It was only when I informed him that there were some young nurses and nutritionists there that he changed his tune. On a previous occasion two young women had gone to do an assessment in Nyamlel and had then walked for hours through flooded areas to carry out assessments in Marial Bai. Dale had

picked them up from the airstrip in Marial Bai and when he flew over the flooded area and saw what they had walked through, he had been impressed. He would do something to help the nurses and nutritionists – the doctor he wasn't too bothered about.

THE PLANNING

Dale flew several types of aircraft, but his favourite was a small Antonov that could carry approximately fourteen hundred kilos of cargo. A truck with wings was how he described the Antonov. It had two doors like bomb doors in the underside of the plane. When these doors were opened a small ladder was lowered to facilitate getting on and off. Dale's plan was to remove the bomb doors, load the plane with supplies and drop out the supplies over Ajiep. We agreed that a few ropes tied around the supplies at the back would stop the goods falling out during take-off. Simple plans are the best.

It all seemed quite simple, anyway, until we got down to planning it in detail. He took off the doors and I gave him a helping hand. He decided that a test flight without the doors would be a good idea and so flew around Loki for a short time. 'Seems OK,' was the answer when he came back.

The next problem was fuel. The Antonov did not have sufficient fuel capacity to do a complete rotation without refuelling, but as he could not land, we had to make other plans. Normally when we flew to a new place for the first time we carried barrels of fuel for refuelling and several 'wet runs' were made to create a fuel dump. On this occasion we would not have spare space for fuel drums, what with all the supplies we intended to drop, and anyway, we could not land. Mike came up with the refuelling solution. The nearest airstrip to Ajiep was a place called Mapel, where the UN had a base. Mike set off to the UN in Loki and enquired about swapping fuel. We would give them several barrels of fuel in Loki and they would make the same quantity available to Dale in Mapel. The refuelling problem was solved.

It was a Saturday when we informed the team in Ajiep that the solution was for the goods to be dropped from the plane

Mr Ray Would Like a Monkey

onto the flooded airstrip, as the water would cushion the blow of the falling sacks. We were thrilled that a solution was in sight and the drop was scheduled for the following day, Sunday. However, later in the day, Dale appeared and said that he needed to talk to us. He indicated that he would use two other pilots, Vladimir (from Russia) and Alec (from Ukraine) to fly the plane and that he would drop the supplies out the back, but that fourteen hundred kilos was a lot for one person to be throwing out of a plane onto a short airstrip. It would take too long, even though the goods were packed into sacks where possible. The time over the airstrip would only be seconds and so a lot of passes over the strip would have to be made and this would use up a considerable amount of fuel. He insisted that he needed somebody from Concern with him. He also reminded us that he needed someone to sign the delivery dockets to say that the goods had been delivered. We had been very strict on the paperwork and did not pay for rotations until we had confirmation of delivery. He was throwing our own rules back at us and smiling! Mike looked at me and shook his head from side to side.

He wanted to know if this was a good idea, but my reply was that it was the only idea we had at the moment, and Dale seemed confident that it would work. And so I agreed to go with Dale – flying in a plane with no doors, piloted by a Russian and a Ukrainian, into South Sudan. There was no chance of getting bored on this job.

THE AIR DROP

Next morning found us up at the airstrip and checking out the best way to secure ourselves in the plane while heaving sacks out the back. There were a lot of people about who were interested in this new idea and were watching everything carefully. Dale had some long webbing straps and he attached one around the base of one of the pilot's seats and then extended it until he was just beside the open doorway at the back. He made a great show of how the webbing had to be locked in position and gave a running commentary to the crowd as he wrapped the webbing around his waist. He then leaned out over the doorway to demonstrate how it worked and immediately fell out and flat on his face. The webbing had not been locked properly. There were roars of laughter as he picked himself up out of the dust. 'Better not do that over Ajiep or you'll be walking back,' was the smart comment from one of the spectators and Dale used some choice words to say what he thought of that. The second time he latched the webbing belt together properly and threw his full weight against it, and it held. Next it was my turn and I made sure that my belt was well and truly anchored and that it closed properly around my waist.

Accompanied by a lot of chatter and laughter, the plane was loaded. Just then a guy from MSF in Loki appeared with a cool box and asked if I could include it in the drop. It was taped up with MSF tape and I was told that the contents were vegetables, including carrots. Nothing surprised me anymore. Now we were going to throw carrots into South Sudan.

The flying time to Ajiep was two and a half hours. We took off from Loki and headed towards our destination. All was well for a short time. The temperature in Loki had been around 47 degrees centigrade and so I was dressed in my usual shorts, lightweight shirt and boots, but very quickly I realised that I was not appropriately attired. As we gained height the temperature dropped right down and soon I was freezing. I was sitting on top of the sacks of supplies and the sacks were feeling colder by the minute. Dale was complaining that he had not thought about how cold it would be without the doors. Among the supplies were sacks with blankets, so we set about cutting open a sack, getting some of the blankets out and wrapping ourselves up in them. Vladimir and Alec seemed to be OK and not suffering from the cold like we were, but as they spoke very little English it was sometimes difficult to know what they felt. Meanwhile we flew on.

Dale and I were chatting, or rather shouting to one another over the noise and he enquired what I would be doing at this time on a Sunday morning if I was back in Ireland. I replied that I would be sitting safely in an armchair reading the Sunday newspapers.

Mr Ray Would Like a Monkey

He shook his head and said that he would find that boring and what we were doing was much more interesting. I had to agree that the job that day was not boring, but I did wonder if I was starting to buy in to the Loki madness. The scenario that I was involved in was not something that I could ever have imagined.

I asked Dale at what height we would come in over the flooded airstrip when doing the drop. He said that he had thought a lot about that detail and had decided that we would come in at six metres. I thought I had misheard him with all the engine and wind noise and shouted,

'Did you say 60 metres?'

'No, six metres, or twenty feet, if you like.'

He laughed and said that if we fell out we would not have far to fall. I was not sure if he was joking or not! We chatted a bit more and eventually lapsed into silence. I was wrapped up in my blankets when I heard a shout from up front. Alec looked back at us, held up five fingers and then made a diving motion with his hand – five minutes to the drop zone.

The plan was to fly over Ajiep once so that people on the ground would know that we had arrived and then circle and come in for the first drop. Dale and I positioned ourselves beside the open doorway from where we could see the ground flying by underneath, backwards. It was a very strange sensation, but quite exciting. I checked my webbing belt a few times and decided it was OK. The plane came in low and Alec shouted 'Snap' at us. Dale started heaving sacks at me and shouted to throw them out, and I heaved them out the back of the plane. After what seemed like only a few seconds the plane nosed upwards very sharply and I heard Alec shout 'Snap, snap' and I stopped heaving the sacks out. The strain on my legs was unbelievable and my stomach felt like I was on a rollercoaster.

'I wish that goddamn commie would speak English,' was the sudden comment from Dale.

All I could do was laugh. We turned in a semi-circle and came back in for the second pass. This time I was ready and when Alex shouted I started heaving the sacks out again as Dale kept passing them to me quickly. In this way we worked our way through the pile of sacks. The MSF cool box went out in the middle of the sacks. It took five passes to get all the supplies out and when the last sack was gone, I breathed a sigh of relief. I was on my knees, exhausted, and my fingers were rubbed raw from the rough sacks. I was covered in sweat, but happy. It was a logistics problem I had been told. Well, logistics had delivered, literally.

We had delivered, but next we needed to take on fuel or we would not get too far. Dale enquired where we were refuelling. I was not sure if he was winding me up, but I told him Mapel. 'Never been there,' was the reply and when he shouted 'Mapel!' to Alec and Vladimir they both shrugged and shook their heads.

'Don't worry,' said Dale, 'There will be a UN flag flying there, so we will find it sooner or later.' We flew in ever-increasing circles looking for a UN flag and sure enough within fifteen minutes we saw the compound, did a pass over the airstrip and then came in to land. We were greeted by a smiling logistician who indicated that he had fuel for us and enquired if we would like lunch. Sunday lunch out, just what we needed. Alec and Vladimir supervised the refuelling and then a Sunday lunch of rice and some goat meat was duly served. We were asked to sign for the lunch, to keep the records straight, and sure enough sometime later a bill came in to Concern from the UN for lunches served in Mapel. We were just finishing lunch when a man called Hugh approached us and said that he was from Oxfam and asked if he could have a lift back to Loki. Dale looked at me and said that as it was a Concern charter, it was up to me. 'No problem,' I said, 'but it could be a bit cold as there are no doors on the plane.' Hugh laughed, presumably thinking that I was just another crazy from Loki. When he arrived at the plane and saw that there really were no doors he seemed a bit shocked and asked where the doors were.

'In Loki,' was Dale's curt reply.

'But why?' asked Hugh.

'It goes faster with no doors.'

After that Hugh asked no more questions about the plane, but he had a puzzled look on his face.

Mr Ray Would Like a Monkey

When I got back to Loki I went to see Mike. He was relieved it was all over. He advised that MSF had been on to the office and they had got the money. I told him that I knew nothing about money and he told me that MSF had needed money on the ground to pay the local staff and had decided to send it in the cool box, but had kept us in the dark.

'By the way, I got your message in my diary,' he said. 'Not funny'.

He seemed a bit annoyed with me but I just laughed. As it was Mike who recorded all the details of goods transported into his diary, I knew that he would record the time of take-off and destination. For a joke, I had written on that day's page that if the mission went pear-shaped, I wanted inscribed on my tombstone; 'He felt sure that it would work.' The exercise proved worthwhile and was repeated on several other occasions by Dale and his team, but I just made the one flight in the door-less plane. Once was enough!

THE BBC

Sometime later we were informed that a team from the BBC were coming out to Kenya and Sudan to make a documentary on our work. The programme was to be called *PK in Sudan* and Patrick Kielty, the comedian, was starring in it. A budget was indicated and I was asked, along with Richard, to draw up a schedule of places to visit and to arrange the logistics. We were advised to keep in mind the security situation in each place. The team duly arrived in Nairobi and we went through the itinerary. There was a lot of laughing at first, as tends to happen when working with a real-life comedian. Security briefings were carried out, as was done for all new arrivals, and people started to get a bit more serious. Part of the security briefing was that all flight times were in Kenya time. This was now indicated in writing on the security document, which was issued to all new staff and visitors after the Tonge mix-up. After a short time in Nairobi we flew down to Loki. I brought the team around the airstrip in Loki to watch the last planes returning from Sudan as dusk was falling. I could see that they were captivated by all the activity. One of the BBC crew commented that he wished he had my job and I was really flattered, but then told him that I would not swap it for anything else. I was really in my element.

The plan for the BBC had been carefully considered and the most suitable plane selected. I informed the team where they would be dropped in Sudan and how long they would stay in each location. They seemed happy enough until I got to the part where I advised them of the day and time that the plane would pick them up again. 'What do you mean pick us up again, is the plane not staying with us?' I was asked. I explained that the plane would be delivering food and medicines, and the details of how rotations worked, and that not a minute was wasted when it came to flying, and they agreed that this was of course necessary. Mike and Richard were going to accompany them and I was in Loki to coordinate matters from there. The first problem that they ran into could have been their last.

A radio message had been sent to the first location to be visited and the ETA of the flight was passed on. Unfortunately, the person taking the message noted down the ETA in the radio log but did not note that the time was in Kenya time. The flight was due at 1000 hours Kenya time but this was 0900 hours in Sudan, so the locals were informed that a plane was due in at 1000 hours. When I was told afterwards I shuddered just thinking about what could have happened. There were anti-aircraft guns located near the airstrip and as the noise of the plane in the distance was heard the gunners started to run towards the guns. They were stopped by our team before they got to the guns, but once again the danger of getting the two time zones mixed up was brought home. Patrick and the team were informed of the mix-up and took it all in good spirit, but after that the ETA times were radioed ahead as normal but with the time in Kenya time and South Sudan time. More lessons learned.

The detailed plan worked well for the first few days, but then word came in that one area to be visited had been bombed and that a change in plan would be a good idea. This seemed simple enough until the matter of the length of airstrip was factored in. The plane that we had booked could not use the new location and so a different plane had to be booked. We did a swap and ended up using the plane that had been booked for the BBC on rotations with supplies and used a supplies plane for the BBC. I had to radio Richard in Sudan and advise that due to technical reasons we had to revise the travel itinerary. He copped on very quickly and there was no panic of any kind. The BBC were in very good hands.

While all this was going on, we were still up to our eyes in rotations, sometimes loading trucks at night-time and getting the goods ready to load into planes for the first rotations. I recall the week of the BBC visit as being remarkably busy. I was living in the Madd House terrace and the guy in the room next to me was the fueller for 748 Air Services. His job was to make sure that planes were re-fuelled when required. The planes were not normally re-fuelled after the last rotation, but instead just before the first rotation well before daylight. Mohammed was the name of the fueller. We got on well together and when he left in the early hours of the morning to go to the airstrip his door made a loud bang. This was my alarm clock call and so I would get up a few minutes after he left. At this stage I was fairly exhausted, with all that was going on and had gone to bed early, before 9 p.m. I was in a deep sleep when I heard Mohammed's door bang. I dragged myself out of bed, pulled on my clothes and boots and headed out into the compound. I went to the office and opened up. A few minutes later, the compound guard appeared with his AK-47 and enquired what was up. I informed him that I was getting ready to do the radio call for the first rotation. He looked at me as if I was crazy. I had the feeling that something was wrong and only then did I look at my watch. It was just after midnight. I went back to bed. I discovered the next day that Mohammed had been up in the UN compound with some friends and had come back late, and it was the door slamming as he came in that had woken me. I was beginning to feel that I needed a break and that some R&R would not go amiss.

R&R

Richard and Mike returned to Loki with the BBC and a short time later Richard and I headed back to Nairobi with the BBC team. They were exhausted, happy, but also a little subdued because of what they had experienced. After a quick wash, the team headed out to Jomo Kenyatta airport for their flight back to London. Meanwhile, Richard informed me that he was going on R&R the next day to the island of Lamu, which is situated in the Indian Ocean off Mombasa. He was going from Friday to Monday and was looking forward to the few days' break. The next morning on the way to the office I said that I wished I was going with him, as I had now worked for 50 days nonstop and was feeling worn out. A quick decision was made and we agreed that we would go to Lamu together. The next four days were just fantastic. We slept a lot and had nice food and fresh fruit. It was great to be away from all the stress, but after a few days the lure to get back to the job was something that could not be resisted. I missed all the activity and was glad to be back in action again.

UN DAILY BRIEFING

Each evening in Loki, at 1830 hours, a briefing was held at UN headquarters. It was held in the open air and was a good way of meeting up with people from the UN and other agencies. Lots of agreements were reached at these times, resulting in the dropping off of supplies at various locations for other NGOs, as well as arranging lifts for people who wanted to travel on one of our rotations. Mike was an expert at networking and persuading people to do favours for us. The meeting followed the same format each evening, with information on the number of UN rotations or sorties flown that day, the total tonnage of food dropped from the UN C-130s and an update on the security situation in South Sudan. I enjoyed the buzz that these meetings generated.

During the period following the end of the Second World War, the greatest airlift in history took place when Berlin was blockaded from receiving supplies by road and all essential items were flown into Berlin by the US Air Force and the RAF. I was at a security briefing one evening when it was reported that the total tonnage dropped in Operation Lifeline Sudan had now exceeded the total tonnage brought in during the Berlin airlift. I had read of the Berlin airlift and the fact that I was in Loki when history was being created made me feel very privileged. All of this of course was not cheap and it was estimated that the cost for aid to South Sudan was approximately one million dollars per day, when all the costs were added up. Large-scale aid does not come cheap.

Bahr el Ghazal

I was informed by the country director that there were some problems in one of our centres in Nyamlel in the province of Bahr el Ghazal and that I needed to visit the place as soon as possible. Nyamlel was a long way from Loki and it took over two and a half hours to fly there. It was situated close to a railway line that ran from North to South Sudan. The railway line played an especially important part in the war. The war was waged by the Northern forces using aerial bombardment from planes and by ground attacks launched, in the main, from the railway.

Southeast of Nyamlel was the town of Wau. This was a government garrison town and the railway was the means by which troops and supplies were transported. There were several trains, all of which were armoured and had artillery on board, as well as troops and horses. Attacks were launched on various towns and villages from the trains. It seemed strange to me to be in a place where there were no proper roads, just dirt tracks, and yet a railway existed that was being used in such a devastating way.

The Concern operation in Nyamlel was being run by a young American nurse who was working under terrible pressure, as she had been on her own for a while, apart from the local staff. Her co-worker was temporarily away on sick leave. I was asked to check out the situation and see what could be done to ease some of the pressure. Sometimes a few simple changes in the logistics process can make life much easier. However, I learned very quickly that a day in Nyamlel threw up problems of all sorts, and that as soon as you sorted out one problem there seemed to be another few just waiting to pop up.

JUSTIN

Nyamlel is situated in a lovely green area overlooking a winding river. My first impression as we came in to land was that it looked idyllic. I was met at the airstrip by a very tall Sudanese man who informed me that his name was Justin and that he would be my interpreter and liaison person with the local community. He introduced me to our bodyguard, who was armed with an AK-47 assault rifle. The local Sudanese Concern staff were able to speak English, but as they were sorting out many issues and moving around a lot the plan was that Justin would help me when required. Although I was informed that his name was Justin, this was more than likely an anglicised version of his real name. I never thought to enquire further, which probably indicates my state of mind at that time. He took me by the hand and led me from the airstrip down towards the Concern compound. He told me that he was available whenever I needed to go anywhere. We were walking along holding hands and this felt a bit strange to me – I could not recall anything like this in my various training days, but as it seemed to be the norm I just went with it. Later I discovered that it was all quite normal and that male friends here walked around holding hands all the time. For an Irishman, it took a bit of getting used to.

As we were walking to the Concern compound lots of children, some obviously malnourished, crowded around us shouting, 'kawaga, kawaga.' I thought that this was very nice as it sounded to me like they were saying, 'How you are, how are you.' So I just smiled at them, shouted 'kawaga' and waved back. There were a lot of mud huts about and the local women smiled and shouted 'kawaga' too. I felt that I was really being welcomed in a big way and felt very much at home. The next morning I was going through the village with Justin and when the locals waved and shouted, 'kawaga,' I waved back and called out 'kawaga' at

Mr Ray Would Like a Monkey

the top of my voice again, and on each occasion this got me a big smile. It seemed that everyone was welcoming me. It was great to be so popular! Justin eventually stopped and asked me why I was calling out 'kawaga' to everyone I met. I told him that I was greeting the locals in the same way that they were greeting me.

'They think that you are very funny,' he said, 'and they like people who are funny, but do you know what "kawaga" means?' he asked.

'Hello, or how you are?' I replied.

'No,' he said, 'it means "white man", so there is no need for you to go through the village announcing "white man, white man". They can see that you are a white man and as there is not another white man around here, there is no need to keep on telling them.'

I felt like a bit of a fool, but then he smiled and said, 'You will be safe here. They feel that you are very funny or just mad, but either way, they like you.'

I was accepted, which is a situation that is not always easy to achieve.

HOME COMFORTS

I initially set up my tent overlooking the river but was informed that this was not advisable for security reasons. There was an old building that had been damaged by bombing and which we used as an office and a store. This too seemed like a good place for my tent, but I was told that the rats would keep me awake at night as they ran up and down the outside of it. Eventually I set up my tent in the middle of our compound, away from the river and the store. My tent was a two-man dome tent that was easily set up in a few minutes. It came with separate layers, an inner one that was ventilated like a mosquito net, and an outer one that was waterproof. I did not use the outer layer, as I was not expecting rain and at night a light breeze would blow through it and I could lie back and see thousands of stars. I had a Walkman (this was the time before iPods) and a few cassettes of my favourite music. Lying in my tent at night, listening to the Eagles or U2, I felt that

I had a set-up that was really hard to beat. I felt quite contented. Daytime was a different story, but it was nice to relax at night.

A GIFT

I had brought some tinned food with me, which consisted mainly of tuna and spam. I was fed up at this stage with the diet in Loki and Sudan. We used water treatment tablets to treat the drinking water, which meant that it had a terrible taste but was potable. I had also brought a box of cornflakes from Nairobi. As there was no such thing as fresh milk, we had powdered milk and I mixed it with the treated water and used the mixture as substitute milk on my cornflakes. This caused diarrhoea at times, but I was determined at this stage to normalise my situation as much as possible and cornflakes for breakfast went a long way toward achieving this normalisation as far as I was concerned.

I kept working on the different issues to be resolved and, apart from my cornflakes, lived off tuna and spam. A UN plane came in one day and a logistician from the UN World Food Programme (UNWFP) came to our compound. He was there to organise a drop zone for a food drop nearby and asked if he could set up his tent in our compound. Before an air drop takes place, the drop zone is clearly marked on the ground. Arrangements are then made with the locals to clear the area of people during the drop, and then collect and store the supplies. The UN organised the distribution of the supplies involved, so there was quite a lot of logistical work involved before the drop actually took place.

It was the practice for a visitor to a compound to bring a small gift with them when they arrived, usually a bottle of Coca Cola or the like, which was always gratefully received. On this occasion the visitor brought me a present of a sandwich from Loki and as he handed it over to me he enquired if I liked tuna. I did not have the heart to tell him that I was already practically living on tuna but, in spite of that, it was genuinely nice. These days I don't really go much for tuna sandwiches!

Mr Ray Would Like a Monkey

THE MEDICAL CENTRE

In Nyamlel word spread very quickly that there was a new boy in town. Justin told me that there was a medical centre nearby that was run by a local medical assistant and that he would like to meet me. A medical assistant (MA) is a medical grade or level that is not seen in Europe. The person involved is not a doctor but is more highly qualified than a local nurse. The MA wanted to see me to discuss some arrangements for Unimix to be supplied directly to the centre, rather than having it all issued through Concern. Unimix, as mentioned earlier, is a fortified food, very like porridge in appearance, and was used extensively in our programmes. We had arranged distributions in different areas around Nyamlel. With the number of places requiring food increasing, it was difficult to meet demand. We needed to revise the overall plan and explore the option of distributing some food through the medical centre.

I was asked by the MA if I would like to visit the centre to see it in operation and gladly accepted the invitation. I had at this stage been trained in advanced first aid as part of my new training schedule, so I was very keen to see what I could learn that might be of use to me in the field. The centre consisted of a brick-built building with every second brick omitted, resulting in a waffle-type construction. This provided essential ventilation in the 45-degree heat. I was lucky that the MA spoke English and he invited me to sit in on medical consultations. I made a record of the various complaints so that I would have information to relay back to our office. It was essential to have as much information as possible to make a case for providing medical supplies as well as food to the centre. Most cases were malaria and were treated with drugs.

The conditions in the building were very basic. It consisted of two rooms, the waiting/treatment area and the pharmacy. There was no electricity and the floor was just compacted clay. The MA sat at a desk in the treatment section and the patients sat around the wall of the building on bench seats. He took the patients' history and if the diagnosis was malaria or another medical condition, he issued details of the drugs to be supplied and the patient went to the room next door to obtain the drugs from the pharmacy, if they were available.

A man came up to the desk and spoke to the MA, who then leaned over to me and said that the patient had complained of blood in his urine. The MA enquired when the problem had started and the patient told him that the blood had appeared three days previously. The patient was wearing a long white shift and he was told to get up onto the examination table to be examined. The MA lifted up the shift and revealed a small hole to one side of the patient's abdomen. He asked him what had happened and the man said that he had recently been shot. I was standing at the MA's shoulder and each time the patient answered he translated straight away. He told me that he was going to ask him exactly when he had been shot.

'Would you like to have a guess as to when it was?'

'Three days ago,' I replied.

It turned out that this was correct. The patient had not made the connection between being shot and the blood in his urine and thought that he had some sort of infection.

Another man brought his young son into the room. The boy had an abscess on his lower back. It was the size of a tennis ball and looked terribly painful. The boy was terrified of course and when he saw me he started to scream. The MA told me not to worry, but that the boy had never seen a white man before as he had just come in from the bush. I knew that the abscess would have to be lanced and enquired about some local anaesthetic. They did not have any. It would have to be lanced with a scalpel as soon as possible and drained. I was asked to help by holding down the child. When the father realised what was about to happen he argued with the MA and the MA said that the father wanted to stop the procedure and leave. He suggested that I tell the father that it was necessary for the lancing to be carried out.

'He might take the advice of a white man,' said the MA.

Mr Ray Would Like a Monkey

I spoke to the man and the MA interpreted. Eventually we held the boy down while an X-shaped incision was made in the abscess and the puss squeezed out. The poor child nearly passed out and was sobbing. A thin bandage soaked in iodine was placed in the wound and gradually removed over several days. The X cut prevented the wound closing up too fast and allowed the gradual removal of the bandage. I was told afterwards that the boy made a full recovery, but I wondered how long it would be before he trusted a white man again.

Later the same morning an exhausted man arrived at the clinic carrying his young son. The father looked like he was about to collapse and the child was emaciated and listless. The MA immediately brought them in and examined the child. The man explained that he had walked through the bush for three days and that the child was the last survivor in his family. His wife and his other children had died and he was afraid that the little boy was going to die too. The MA showed me how to check the child for dehydration and we found he was severely dehydrated, as well as being very malnourished. One of the signs of malnourishment is what is called 'old man's face,' where a child looks like an old man. Another sign is that hair turns orange. This child had all these signs. His breathing was laboured and the MA told me that he also had pneumonia. He then wrote down the patient's name, Perdi, and his age, and asked me to get in touch with Loki to see if I could arrange a medevac for the child.

I made my way back to the Concern compound and got on the radio straight away. I passed on the details and was told to wait while it was checked out. A nurse from the Red Cross hospital in Loki told me that a medevac could not be approved as the terms of reference were that they only took war-wounded, or dependents of war-wounded. The only way that approval could be given would be if the child's father was classified as war-wounded. I returned to the medical centre and informed the MA, who passed on the message to the father. The father started to cry and I felt terrible about being the bearer of such bad news. The MA and the father had a discussion that was not immediately translated for me. The MA looked at me and asked for confirmation that there would be no problem with a medevac if the father was a war victim and wounded. I agreed that that was how I saw it. The father looked at me and spoke in a pleading voice. The MA then said to me, 'He wants to be shot in the foot. Will you do it?' To be honest I was tempted, but felt that it would not have a good outcome overall, and so I refused to have anything to do with shooting the father, even if it was just in the foot. When the MA told the father that there would be no medevac, the father took my hand and thanked me for trying. I felt really terrible that there seemed to be so little that we could do but we discussed what other options might be open to us. The MA said that what was needed was antibiotics and rehydration by IV, but he had no IV lines.

Both the child and his father also needed food, and this we had. I returned to the compound and asked our nurse what we could provide and was told that the Concern programme was to provide food, but we did not have what was required medically. She gave me the key to the store and I got a quantity of Unimix and headed back to the medical centre with some of our local staff. Emotions were running a bit high on all sides at this stage and the father was just sitting in the dust, crying.

We handed over the Unimix to some of the local women and the MA asked them to mix it with hot water and give it to the father and some to Perdi, if he would take it. The MA gave us some rehydration fluids and antibiotics and asked if we could give the fluids and antibiotics to the child by mouth when required. He showed us the quantity of fluids to give and warned us not to exceed the dose, because if we did, it could be fatal. He advised us not to get our hopes up, as it was quite likely that little Perdi would die soon. We agreed that the medicines and fluids would be given as scheduled and hoped for the best. Two days later Perdi was sitting in our arms and starting to feed himself with Unimix from a bowl. He survived. I don't know why, but I kept the slip of paper with the request for the medevac from the MA. Maybe it was just to remind me that you should not give up too

Mr Ray Would Like a Monkey

easily and that while there is life, there is hope. However, the fragile balance between life and death was brought home to me just a few days later.

A group of boys were playing with a football in the village near our compound in the middle of the day. The 'ball' consisted of a bunch of rags tied together with string and they were obviously enjoying themselves. Around 5 p.m. that evening some of the locals came to us and asked us to see a sick boy. I think that after the miracle of Perdi, they thought that we could do anything. One of the boys who had been playing football a few hours earlier was extremely sick, so we immediately went to get the MA. He examined the boy, who by this time was foaming at the mouth and whose eyes were rolling in his head. The MA diagnosed cerebral malaria and treated him, but within a few hours the boy had died. A malnourished child has little chance of surviving cerebral malaria.

CROCODILE MAN

A few days later, a man appeared in our compound and said that a friend out in the bush had lost his leg due to a crocodile biting him. I asked how he was and he replied that his friend was OK but asked if we could get him out to Loki.

When taking a patient's history, several specific questions are asked using acronyms as a guide, so that you don't leave out vital information. However, as I was not out in the bush with the patient, I made the mistake of taking the information at face value from the friend. I was more focused on using the correct terminology to see if I could get medevac approval from Loki, than I was focused on the patient. I called in on the radio and described the problem as a traumatic amputation and then, when asked for more detail, reluctantly advised that the cause of the amputation was a crocodile. It could not be described as a war wound unless the croc was working for the Northern forces, but I was still hopeful. I was asked the time of the event and I had to admit that I had not enquired.

'Come back to us when you find out,' was the curt reply.

I asked the messenger when the incident had occurred and was told that the leg had been bitten off over twenty years earlier. Fooled again!

It appeared that several requests had been put in to Loki at different times for crocodile man to be medevaced. I was not the first to be made a fool of and I heard afterwards that I was not the last. He was not airlifted out.

LOOKS LIKE RAIN

The local team had a great sense of humour and after the *kawaga* episode when I first arrived, were convinced that I loved a joke too. The weather had been particularly good in Nyamlel and I had been sleeping without the waterproof cover over my tent. I went to bed one night and listened to my Walkman but could hear rumbling in the distance. When there were some flashes in the sky I thought that a bad thunderstorm was on the way. I got out of the tent and started to put the waterproof cover over it. The local team, who were sitting around chatting, saw this and asked what I was doing.

'Putting up the waterproof cover before the rain appears,' was my reply. They roared laughing as if I had made a very humorous comment. They told me that it was not going to rain for weeks, but I imagined that I would have the last laugh when the thunderstorm came, so I completed the task and went back to bed. I went to sleep fairly quickly, only to be woken by one of the team telling me to get up, as we had to move. Thinking that this was another of their jokes, I told them to go away, but quickly realised they were serious. The thunder sounds were louder now and they told me the noise was from guns being fired. That woke me up! The armoured train was on the move and firing into the night. We needed to get ready to move out if necessary. After a while, the situation eased and the noise died down.

Next morning at 0430 hours I had to do a radio call to Loki to inform Mike of the situation. I was not allowed to use the word 'guns' over the radio, but still had to get a clear message through to him. After informing him of the weather, the next item on the agenda was the security situation. As he was keen on sailing I thought that a reference to boats would be the best approach for getting my message across. I enquired if he had ever taken part in yacht- racing in Ireland and when he came back with a hesitant, 'Affirmative, what has that got to do with anything?' I enquired if he recalled how they started races at home. Yacht races are started by the firing of a cannon or a loud bang and this registered with Mike.

'Well,' I informed him, 'We had a few yacht races here last night, but all is calm this morning.' He became quite worried, but as the train with the guns had obviously moved on it was no longer a problem. He was unsettled though, because he was on the radio several times during the day, enquiring if there were any more yacht races. I am sure that anyone listening in on the radio would have been convinced that the Irish guys had finally lost their marbles.

Many years later I met some people in Zimbabwe who had just moved from Nyamlel. They informed me that some of the local team were still there and had told them the story of the night that an Irishman had put a waterproof cover over his tent for protection from the guns. They thought this was very funny. Only I knew better!

When I returned to Loki a few days later, I was told that the UN security officer wanted to see me without delay. They wanted to discuss the heavy gunfire that I had heard a few days earlier. At this stage I was covered in dust, had not shaved for some time and wanted to get cleaned up first, but I was whisked up to UN HQ and debriefed. It turned out to be quite a pleasant experience, as the UN security officer had spent some time in Northern Ireland years before and we ended up having a chat about different places there. I was also pleased that somebody was actually interested in what I had to say about the situation that I had just experienced. I felt that I now belonged, albeit in a small way, to the massive programme that was Operation Lifeline Sudan.

SATELLITE TV

Like most capital cities in the world, Nairobi had a few shopping centres plus restaurants, bars and cinemas. Occasionally I would go to the cinema when I was in Nairobi and it was nice to have time to chill out. For the people working in Sudan there was little in the form of entertainment, even if they had time to relax. Work and sleep were the order of the day there.

Loki, however, was the halfway house between Sudan and Kenya and the business opportunities it provided had not gone unnoticed by the business people in Nairobi. There were a few shanty bars in mud huts, but the best place in town was the compound called Kate Camp. It had a good restaurant and bar and did bed and breakfast in tented accommodation. The UN compound had a canteen where the food was good and they also had a bar. These were the places where networking could be done at night-time. Mike was the expert networker and many a plan was hatched in Kate Camp or the UN compound. I was not into networking in the same way as Mike was and preferred to just rest for an hour or so in the evening and try to forget about all the activity.

Satellite TV is now an everyday thing, but when we first moved into Loki it was a huge bonus. A large TV was located in an open-sided tent in the UN compound. The viewing area was laid out with plastic chairs lined up on each side of a central aisle. Saturday night was the night when people gathered to watch TV. All was proceeding nicely one evening when suddenly there were shouts and people started jumping from their seats. A snake was coming down the central aisle and heading towards the TV. There were shouts of 'Snake, snake!' and the African staff quickly attacked and killed the offender. The international staff were afraid of snakes and moved away, whereas the African staff, although afraid, would attack with ferocity. Within seconds it was dead and people were retaking their seats when someone called out that the audience was overreacting and the snake just wanted to see what was the latest on Sky news. Loki wit in action.

DALE MISSING

Rotations from Loki were booked on a monthly basis with several charter companies. We estimated how many hours' flying time we needed for each type of aircraft, bearing in mind the length of the airstrips at each location. We had agreed a lot of rotations with 748 Air Services (748AS) and were on target. We did not have rotations every day but worked to a schedule that was updated each week. Flexibility was the name of the game. As other NGOs needed flying access to Sudan, the rotations were strictly allocated and if for any reason we missed our slot, our rotation was gone. One evening goods had been put by for loading on the next morning's first rotation when Mike informed me that Dale was stuck in Sudan and would not make it back to Loki that night. He had been delayed during the day and it was too late for him to take off as it would be dark when he arrived back in Loki and he could not land in the dark. The absence of landing lights at Loki was a real impediment. I was a bit put out as this would screw up our rotations for the next day. If we missed the first slot we had to wait until it was our turn again, but Mike informed me that Dale was apologetic and said that he would not let us down. He had a plan.

'Here we go again!' I thought.

He had told Mike that he would take off in the dark in Sudan and would be back in Loki by daylight, in time to load for the first rotation. He had made arrangements for a barrel with a fire in it to be placed at the end of the airstrip in Sudan, and he would use that as a reference for take-off instead of landing lights.

'The man is definitely mad!' I thought, and was a bit worried until I heard that Dale had done that sort of thing before.

We got up early next morning and went to the airstrip in Loki to await Dale's arrival. We had received information on the radio that Dale had taken off, was on his way to us and should be with us shortly after 0600 hours. All the planes had taken off from Loki by 0630 hours and we waited and waited. Still no sign of Dale.

We started to get worried, and when several hours had passed Mike became very despondent.

'He's dead, it's the end of him!' said Mike matter-of-factly in his strong Cork accent.

'He did not have enough fuel to be flying for this number of hours.'

Tears gathered in Mike's eyes and I was not far off crying myself. I had thought that Dale was indestructible but was now convinced that he was lying in the middle of the bush in Sudan. We had our breakfast and went back to the office, both of us very dejected.

A while later the radio crackled into life and we heard the voice of the missing airman over the airwaves. He was all apologies. He had taken off in the dark as planned, but a short time later one engine had failed and he had had some electrical problems as well, so he kept circling until he could find a place to land. He had had trouble with the radio due to the electrical problems, but now had that fixed and wanted to talk to his mechanic. Mike was jumping around the place shouting, 'He's alive, he's alive!'

It took several days to get the plane sorted out and another plane and a mechanic had to fly into Sudan with spares before Dale was able to return. When I saw him I told him that I had been convinced that he had died and would have missed him, but he just shrugged and said it was nothing and that he was sorry for screwing up the rotations. Same old, same old. He was back.

FREE FLIGHTS

The planes we used would sometimes fly without cargo between Loki and Nairobi to be serviced. This procedure was known as positioning of aircraft. We chartered planes from several aircraft companies and had an arrangement with them that when planes were positioning we would be told in advance. As the planes were empty we could hitch a free ride on them. The alternative was to pay for flights on passenger-carrying planes.

I was in Loki and had arranged to travel on a free flight to Nairobi. The plane was full and we were getting ready to leave

Mr Ray Would Like a Monkey

when a woman from the International Committee of the Red Cross (ICRC) came on board and asked if there was a spare seat for a person who was sick and needed to go to hospital. All the seats were taken, so she asked if anyone was willing to give up their seat and promised that she would arrange a free flight on an ICRC plane that was going to Nairobi the following morning. I agreed to give up my seat and she thanked me and advised that she would be in our compound the next day with my travel pass. However, she appeared the next morning looking embarrassed and told me that, as I was not working for ICRC, I could not travel on the plane. She had made the promise in good faith but was restricted by their rules. It seemed that the bigger the organisation, the more rules and regulations applied. I was a bit annoyed as she had promised a free flight and now the cost would have to be met by Concern.

I made contact with our director in Nairobi and asked him if he could influence the situation, but he advised that he could do nothing and that we would have to buy a ticket on the next commercial flight. I was still not happy about the situation, so I went back to the ICRC compound and told them that I was disappointed that, having facilitated them, we would now have to pay for a ticket and that, under the circumstances, perhaps they would consider buying the ticket for me. After all, if I had travelled the previous night, I would have been on a free flight. She agreed that what I proposed was reasonable but replied that although they bought tickets from a commercial airline when required, they purchased the tickets on credit and tickets were only issued against an approved list. I wasn't on the approved list, so she could not get a ticket for me.

After all the wheeling and dealing in Loki, my mind was working a little differently to the way it used to, and 'needs must' was the expression that summed up our approach on many occasions. She obviously wanted to help so I suggested that she purchase a ticket for someone who was on the approved list and then give it to me. When you boarded a plane in Loki no one checked passports and the names of the passengers were just called out.

Having a plane ticket there was similar to having a train ticket at home. Passports were occasionally checked in Nairobi, but as the flight was internal (Loki to Nairobi), it was just as likely that there would be no passport check there. So we formed a plan that would probably get me locked up today, given the current security measures. It was all very simple. She bought a ticket for a Swedish aid worker who was on leave. All I had to remember was that when they called out his name, I was to board the aircraft, which I did. When we arrived in Nairobi I was a bit nervous that the deception would be discovered, but no one checked the passport names against the passenger list. I was back in Nairobi free of charge but flying close to the wind.

RUTF

RUTF is an acronym for Ready-to-Use Therapeutic Food and is used to treat severely malnourished children. Our chief medical officer had advised that we needed a type of RUTF called F75 for several locations in Sudan. It was expensive, not readily available in Kenya and had to be imported from Europe. Due to the situation in Sudan the Kenyan government had a policy of fast-tracking goods destined for the famine-stricken areas through customs. In the main, the procedure worked well, but occasionally there were hiccups in getting goods released from customs. The release of the F75 was one of those occasions when someone decided to get awkward.

The internal procedure in Concern for importing goods from overseas was that the country director had to approve the request for the F75 and the Dublin office had to arrange the actual procurement. All of this takes time and so pressure was mounting on the logistics team in Nairobi. Dublin reacted quickly and very soon the F75 arrived at Jomo Kenyatta International Airport. It was then that the problems started. All the paperwork was in order, but when it was submitted to customs there was one query after another. Our local logistician, Judy, was backwards and forwards but getting nowhere. I asked her what the problem was and was told that someone in customs wanted a bribe to release the goods. This we would not do. Money had been donated to feed the starving, not to bribe corrupt officials.

I was getting more and more annoyed at the delay and after a few days told Judy that I was going with her to customs. This suggestion was met with horror.

'If he sees you, he will want even more money,' I was told.

My position was clear, 'He is not getting *any* money so *more* does not come into the equation.'

I travelled out to the airport the next morning with Judy and told her that I would give her some time to resolve the problem, but if it was not sorted out soon, I would take over. I waited in the car while negotiations went on, but after some time it became obvious that the official was holding out. The Kenyans have a saying in Swahili, *pole pole* (pronounced poley poley), which means 'slowly slowly' and they are fond of using this expression to describe the ideal way of getting things done. I had heard the expression on numerous occasions when they thought that we were pushing matters along too fast. However, the RUTF had a short shelf life in the heat, so I felt that *pole pole* was not really an option.

When Judy appeared, looking worried, I asked her to take me to see the official. I was introduced and asked him to spell his name and position and carefully wrote the details in my notebook. After the formalities were completed, I asked him what the problem was, only to be told that the paperwork was wrong, but he would help to sort it out. I knew that the next question I was expected to ask was how much the help would cost. But I had had enough and asked him if he know who Mr David Andrews was.

He smiled and said, 'No, does he work for Concern?'

'No,' I said, 'He is the Irish Minister for Foreign Affairs and the Irish government have donated money to the Sudan emergency and have financed the product that is held in customs. I am now going back to my office to telephone him, give him your name and tell him that you won't release the goods. I expect that he will telephone your Minister for Foreign Affairs and enquire as to why you are holding matters up. I want you to be clear on what action I am going to take unless the goods are released now.'

Within minutes the papers were stamped and we were on our way.

Sometimes a direct approach works best, but despite getting the goods released I had a nagging feeling that I had dealt badly with the situation.

LOST IN A STORM

Flying over the bush from Nairobi to Loki was exciting at first, but after a while it became routine. The flights left from Wilson airport, a small but extremely busy place. Life had become such that small pleasures were much appreciated and the bonus at Wilson airport was that I could buy sausage rolls and a bottle of Coke before I got on the small plane.

Time in Africa is a bit hit and miss, and sometimes the plane would take off as scheduled and at other times delays were the norm. I had learned to go with the flow as far as timekeeping was involved. The flying time to Loki was nearly two hours and I usually fell asleep shortly after take-off.

I went out to Wilson one morning and was told that there would be a delay as the weather over Loki was bad and a thunderstorm was raging. I had experienced rain in Nairobi but had yet to see it in Loki, where the weather was normally dry and extremely hot, with everyday temperatures of around 47 degrees centigrade. We eventually took off and I dozed. Sometime later I awoke and had a look at my watch. It was nearly time to land and I was waiting for the descent towards the airstrip. I had made the journey so many times that I could normally pick out the various landmarks, but on this occasion was having trouble seeing anything. There were black clouds all around and the weather was more like Ireland than Africa. When I could see the ground it did not look familiar and after a while, I wondered what was going on. We had now been flying for quite a long time. There was no division between the pilots and the passengers, so we were able to ask them what was happening.

'We could not see the ground at Loki, so we are flying over Sudan now and hoping that the clouds will clear at Loki,' was the reply. After a while we banked and the pilot told us that we were headed back towards Loki and would fly in a circle until we could land. This procedure went on for some time. Later one of the pilots asked us to look out the portholes to see if any of us could locate the airstrip, as we were a bit low on fuel. It seemed that passenger participation was now required – not a good sign.

I could see that a few of the passengers were a bit nervous. A woman started to cry and said we would all be killed, whereupon the pilot told her not to worry as we could look out for the only road into Loki and land on the road if we had to. It says something about my state of mind that I then thought that landing on the road seemed like a good idea and was glad of the fact that I had eaten the sausage rolls, as otherwise I would have been quite hungry. I really was becoming quite laissez-faire about situations that I had no control over – or maybe I was just getting crazier by the day.

One of the pilots was telling us how much flying time we had left when the other one let out a shout saying that he could see the airstrip, and we came in to land straight away.

The poor woman who had been nervous was first out the door and vomited on the airstrip right beside the plane. Mike appeared and asked what the holdup had been. When I told him we were lost for a while, he said that he had been waiting ages and had a lot of work to do and was fed up waiting for me. We were both having a bad day it seemed, and now it was bloody raining. Some days just got worse instead of better.

ABORT, ABORT

One morning Mike and I were up at the airstrip, waiting for a plane from 748AS to return to Loki for refuelling and loading. The air traffic control (ATC) at Loki was quite basic. The controller sat up in a wooden box-like structure near the airstrip and directed planes in and out as required. There was no radar or landing lights, so all operations took place in daylight and the controller relied on his eyes, ears and binoculars, along with radio transmissions, to keep track of what was going on. There were mountains north of the airstrip, so planes always took off in a southerly direction to gain sufficient height and then turned north and crossed over the mountains into Sudan. Planes coming back from Sudan could not be seen until they crossed over these mountains and were very close to Loki. There were a few plane wrecks at the edge of the airstrip that reminded us that accidents could and did happen. On the ground we could communicate with the ATC by using our VHF radios, but these radios were not suitable for contacting the planes.

We knew roughly when our plane was due in and were waiting patiently near the edge of the runway for it to arrive. We noticed a plane from the ICRC pulling out from the loading area and making its way towards the northern end of the airstrip, where it would then turn 180 degrees prior to departure. As it passed us, we noticed that the loading doors were still open and we could see several 200-litre barrels of fuel stored in the aircraft. The plane continued to the top of the strip, turned and revved the engines in preparation for take-off, but the doors remained open. As the plane started to roll forward, I realised that the pilot had forgotten to close the doors. I was worried about what could happen during take-off, with all the barrels of fuel on board. If the barrels broke loose we would be in trouble.

We waved frantically at the plane but the pilot seemed to be unaware of the problem. I switched the radio channel to the ATC frequency and called out 'ICRC abort, ICRC abort,' to the controller. The plane, which was now accelerating down the runway, suddenly slowed down and stopped. The controller asked what was wrong and I told him about the open doors. A few seconds later the doors were closed and the plane did another U-turn and headed back up to the northern end of the strip again. The pilot gave us the thumbs up as he taxied past us, then turned and got ready again for take-off.

'He owes me a beer,' I thought.

The engines revved, but as he started to roll forward we heard another plane approaching in the air from the north. The 748AS plane that we had been waiting for was heading into land towards the northern end of the strip. The ICRC plane should have waited until it passed over him and landed, but there had been a breakdown in communications somewhere. We looked on in horror as the 748AS plane approached to land and the ICRC plane moved down the runway for take-off. A crash seemed inevitable and Mike and I started to run away from the strip as fast as we could. Mike was shouting as he ran, 'That Red Cross bastard is going to wreck *our* fucking plane.' It didn't seem like the time to point out to him that it wasn't in fact '*our* fucking plane' as it was on lease, because by that time I was concentrating on running as fast as I could. I looked over my shoulder as the 748AS plane banked like a Spitfire from the Second World War and swept over and then away from the accelerating plane on the airstrip, before eventually going around and coming in to land. The pilot was pale and shaking when he got out of the plane.

'Did you see that?' he shouted, 'he could have killed us all!' We were all shaken up but quickly arranged for the plane to be loaded and re-fuelled. We could not stand around gossiping when there were planes to be loaded with essential supplies, but I knew deep down that it had been a close call and that I for one had just had my biggest fright so far.

BIBLES

Each month Mike and I contacted aircraft leasing companies and booked flying hours for the various rotations. The selection was based on the length of airstrip available to us. When I had first arrived, I naively thought that if we booked bigger planes, we could reduce the number of rotations required, failing to realise that bigger planes needed longer airstrips. I had learned a lot since those first few weeks. The most versatile of the small planes was the Antonov and there were two of these available to us from two different companies, but we had to book the flying hours month by month. We were negotiating hours for the following month when we were told that one of the planes we needed would not be available for all the hours requested. We enquired why this was, as we had so far always booked more or less the same hours each month.

Dale, always the one person whom you could rely on to come up with something different, told us that he had a contract to fly bibles into South Sudan. He went on to explain that some American evangelists had packed bibles into crates and wanted them delivered to Sudan, and that they were willing to pay top rates for the delivery. Mike and I were incredulous and thought that this was another of Dale's jokes.

'They don't need bibles there, they need food!' we shouted, but Dale was unmoved. He could make good money by flying them in and wasn't going to turn down business.

'This place is getting worse,' I thought, and still wasn't sure if it was a wind-up.

However, Dale did fly his cargo of bibles into Sudan. We had had him booked for some rotations later in the week, but then got a message to say that he was stuck in Sudan. The people at his destination were not used to testing the ground to see if the airstrip was landable and the ground was so wet when he landed that the plane buried its nose wheel in the soil.

'Serves him right,' we thought, 'getting involved in harebrained schemes.'

He appeared back in our office in Loki several days later and I was still annoyed with him for losing us valuable rotation time.

'Next time stick with the people who know what they're doing,' I said, but his reply as usual was not what I expected. He went on to explain that the bibles had been made of rice paper. I expected him to say that he and the locals had eaten the bibles, but he went one better.

'Up there', he said, referring to a place in Sudan, 'they had some marijuana plants and I used the rice paper to roll some joints, so while I was waiting for the ground to dry out I was smoking the bibles and everything was cool!'

Once again, he had managed to leave us stuck for words.

PROBLEMS ON ALL FRONTS

I was back working in the office in Nairobi when Kathleen, a young Scottish doctor who had been suffering from malaria, offered to help us in logs while she was recuperating. Nairobi was a lot cooler than Loki and so it was easier for people to regain their strength there when they were recovering from a serious illness. When she had asked if she could help in any way, we were glad of the offer and gave her various jobs checking invoices, delivery dockets and other paperwork, as well as dealing with some of the radio calls. She was interested in how logs functioned and keen to learn as much as she could. It was great having an extra pair of hands, and her Scottish accent was music to my ears. As it turned out, she experienced a week where security issues almost took over logs.

We relied heavily on security information updates for keeping our staff safe. The trains from which attacks were launched in Sudan normally moved at a very slow pace. This was because soldiers often walked in front of them to check that no land-mines or explosives had been laid on the tracks. Whenever we received news of any unusual movement of government forces or their proxies, we took notice. The CD had travelled to Loki on his way into Sudan at this time, so I had the dubious honour of being in overall charge. I received information that there was unusual movement along the railway line that was close to one of our camps and sent a radio message to Mike suggesting a temporary relocation of our staff until matters became clearer. Our primary method of communication was the short-wave radio. We had recently managed to set up email using satellite communication technology between Nairobi and Loki through sat-phones, but it was extremely expensive for verbal communication as well as email. How times have changed.

However, on this occasion I followed up with an email and asked him to get approval for an evacuation from the CD, who was still in Loki. Later in the day I received a message from Mike telling me that the CD had discussed my request with the security people and the decision had been made that an evacuation was not necessary. It seemed that I was worrying unnecessarily. Mike was told to tell me that it was OK and to relax. I didn't feel so sure but left the final decision to the people with more experience than me. This was on a Tuesday afternoon.

On Wednesday morning I was working in the office with Kathleen and the rest of the team when I was told that there was a person from MSF looking for me downstairs. I went down to see them and was then asked if we had an Australian logistician working for us in Sudan. I confirmed that we had and asked what the problem was.

'You need to get him out and back here,' I was told, 'we have some bad news.'

They did not want to tell me what it was, but I said that I could not pull someone out without a bit more information. Eventually they informed me that his partner had been killed in a helicopter crash. She had been working in an emergency situation in Honduras and the helicopter she was in had crashed into the sea. The pilot's body had been recovered, but his partner was missing. Information like this could not be passed on over the radio, as everyone could hear, so I made contact with Mike on the sat-phone. I told him the news and said that he would have to get the logistician out as soon as possible. He indicated that he would change some rotations to facilitate this. I was not looking forward to the next few days.

When I went into work early on the Thursday morning, I could hear the radio barking away with our call sign and the station calling identifying itself as Loki. It was Mike on the radio, sounding worried, and I had a bad feeling. Kathleen followed me into the radio room.

'Are you sitting down?' Mike asked, and I wondered what was up.

'The UN have ordered evacuation from several locations in Sudan,' he said. 'As of 0400 hours this morning the balloon has gone up. They are gathering up people in different locations and flying them to a central collection point in Sudan. As soon as they have them all together, they will start to fly them back to Loki'.

I was stunned but tried to remain cool on the radio. After all, other people could hear the transmission. I enquired if our staff were safe and was told that all were accounted for. They would be flown into Loki and then a decision would be made as to who was going where. Meanwhile, bringing the Australian logistician back to Nairobi and breaking the bad news to him would have to wait. There was a SOP when an emergency security evacuation like this happened, so I had to get in touch with the Dublin office and give them hourly updates. I was very worried but at the same time had to appear unruffled. Our troubles were not over yet.

On Thursday afternoon Kathleen let me know that we had a radio call from a location in Sudan that had not been affected by the evacuation and they wanted to speak to me. The radio operator was very calm and informed us that their area was being bombed from the air! I went into radio speak automatically and informed him, 'We have a good copy', meaning that we were receiving his message clearly.

'Have you any casualties and do you require evacuation?' I asked. I was dreading the answer.

'Negative, they will be gone soon and we can get back to work. Just advising for record purposes'.

I recorded in the radio log that Yankee Echo was being bombed and we had no casualties.

'Anything else to report?' I asked.

'Negative, just looking forward to a beer when we reach your location,' was the reply.

I had to admire his approach as I signed off. He was calmness personified. Kathleen stared at me with a puzzled look on her face.

'What?' I asked.

'What does it take to get you guys excited? Evacuations going on, places being bombed, and it's all 'Good copy' and 'meet you for a beer',' she replied.

'Well, we have to give the impression of being very calm and then hopefully everyone else will be calm. We're a bit like ducks, gliding across the lake but paddling like mad under the water. On the surface there's no fuss'.

By Friday all the evacuees were out of Sudan and in Loki, but the place was overflowing. The Australian logistician had been brought out too by this time. MSF offered to fly him to Honduras but, as he said himself, there was no point – his partner's grave was in a helicopter somewhere in the sea, and he went home. Mike sent me an email in which he still managed some light wit but was obviously much stressed. It was short and to the point:

'I am very tired at the moment and feel a bit like Oscar Schindler with all that's going on AT THE MOMENT. Maybe this nightmare will soon be over.

Mike'

Most of the evacuees stayed in Loki and later returned to Sudan when the situation calmed down. A few came to Nairobi. I met them at Wilson airport on Saturday afternoon and they looked quite shocked. One nurse could best be described as shell-shocked. She had the thousand-yard stare that I had seen in people in Bosnia. She wrapped herself up in a duvet and sat on the sofa in the visitors' apartment and refused to go out.

Kathleen had asked what it was that would get us excited – I found out later that weekend. My way of relaxing was to listen on my Walkman to the tapes that my daughter Jenny had put together for me. We had similar tastes in music, as well as the same sense of humour, and when I listened to the music it reminded me of home and family and helped me to unwind. The tapes had great sentimental value and Jenny had put a lot of time and effort into putting them all together. I was sitting on my own on Sunday, glad of the peace and quiet for once, and inserted a tape into the Walkman. The Walkman chewed up the tape. When I inserted a second tape, the same thing happened, but when it chewed up the third tape, I lost my cool. I fired the Walkman at the wall and it disintegrated. I was on the verge of tears.

'What am I doing'? I thought, 'I've taken everything that was thrown at me this week and now I'm losing the plot over a broken Walkman'.

A few days later I received an email from the Dublin office complimenting Mike and me on how we had handled a tough situation and expressing confidence in us as a team. My reaction was, 'Great, thanks, can I go home now?'

I was feeling the stress, but we still had another month to go.

LOKI MADNESS

It was early December and Mike and I were really feeling the strain. Our sense of humour was becoming more bizarre by the day, just like that of most of the other people in Loki. We came out of the office one Saturday afternoon and found there were some people from MSF nearby. Mike looked up at the sky, clear and blue as usual, the temperature over 45 degrees centigrade.

'Nice day to go sailing,' Mike ventured, 'maybe we should get the boat out?'

The guys from MSF looked at us and Mike started to play to the audience. He elaborated on his 'plans' for the afternoon, which included a picnic and a bit of sailing beyond the harbour and warned that we would have to look out for the south westerlies.

'Right, let's go and get the boat,' he said, and off we trotted to his room and fell about the place laughing.

MSF were totally mystified, as we were in the middle of the bush. Boats and rivers, not to mention the sea, were a long way off. Mike commented that they thought that we were crazy, and I replied that everyone was crazy in Loki and nothing would surprise me anymore.

'It doesn't matter what you do in this place, no one bats an eyelid,' I said.

I referred to the cross-dressing Corporal Klinger in the TV series M*A*S*H and maintained that we could walk around Loki dressed as women and no one would notice. One of the guys in the compound had been shouting at the planes for weeks when they flew overhead, and we had all thought that it was hilarious. It was only when he came out to the compound naked one morning that anybody realised that he had been there too long.

Mike commented on the idea of the cross-dressing but disagreed with me and said that it would definitely get a reaction.

'OK, I'll try it,' I said. 'You buy me a beer if I'm right'.

We went to the store, where we had second-hand clothes in stock for the IDPs in Sudan. I asked for a skirt and a top and Bravo Oscar, aka Ben the storekeeper, refused, saying that he needed a supply request. So off we went to the office, got the required paperwork and returned to the store. We handed in the supply request and waited. Ben asked what colour skirt was required and I told him that I would like a blue one. He handed me the skirt and I tried it on over my shorts and desert boots. It was a good fit. He looked at me and then enquired what colour top I would like. I told him white, and he handed one over. I tried it on and didn't like it as it was too tight, so I gave it back. Ben then asked us to update the paperwork and I deleted the top from the supply request and initialled the change. I was waiting for further comment, but none came.

We then decided that we needed to test our theory in the open and so walked across the compound to our office. We met several people but all we got was 'Hello Romeo Tango, hello Mike Lima,' as they passed us. I felt that I had proved my point at this stage, but Mike thought differently.

'Let's go outside the compound,' he said.

We had two people coming in from Nairobi, so we went up to the airstrip to meet them off the plane. We met various people on the way, but still no one commented on the skirt and just greeted us as usual. When our people from Nairobi arrived at the airstrip the Irish accountant greeted me as normal, but the second person, who was American, asked why I was wearing a skirt. I told her that it was cooler wearing a skirt in Loki and that I was trying to adjust to it. She just smiled. We went back to the compound and I told Mike that he owed me a beer as only one person had commented on the skirt and that person was an American, so it didn't really count as they would comment on anything.

Mr Ray Would Like a Monkey

'OK,' he said, 'we'll go to the UN bar and I'll buy you a beer, but first you have to take off that fucking skirt. It really doesn't suit you.'

When I returned the skirt to the store, I had to fill in all the paperwork for goods returned and that taught me a lesson – don't dream up schemes that involve the storekeeper. No one ever commented directly to my face afterwards, although I am not too sure what they were saying behind my back. Mike thought the whole episode hilarious. Our sense of humour, even if it was a bit bizarre, was just about keeping us going.

RADIO FREE LOKI

We decided that life needed a lift. The constant demands for supplies and the irrational behaviour from some of those on Lariam (a malaria prophylaxis that can cause psychiatric symptoms) had us worn down. We had reached the stage where we thought that everyone was crazy except us, a sure sign that we were stressed as well as exhausted. One morning over a cup of tea we discussed the film *Good Morning Vietnam*, starring Robin Williams, and decided that what we needed in Loki was our own pirate radio station. Mike was a radio buff and I thought that he might be able to get some broadcasting equipment so we could do request shows!

The high frequency (HF) radio we used for long distance transmissions between Loki, Nairobi and Sudan was operated under very strict rules and playing music over it was enough to get you fired and sent home, so using the HF was not an option. We had just completed a stock-take in the store and there were several battery-operated megaphones in stock that were used for making announcements to large groups of IDPs. The battery power amplified the sound so that it travelled some distance. I went back to Nairobi a few days later and while there bought a ghetto blaster radio and tape deck combined. I also bought some cassette tapes with different types of music. When I next returned to Loki, I carried with me the massive radio and the tapes.

When darkness fell, we set up the radio, jammed the switch on the megaphone and welcomed the compound listeners to Radio Free Loki and asked them to send in requests. The sound boomed out over the compound and it wasn't too long before we got a request – to turn the damn thing off. It was bad enough during the day with the noise from all the planes, but now at night-time we were disturbing people, so the pirate station had a very short life! One side effect we had not considered was how the compound residents would react to the different types of music. As it was early December we played some Christmas carols, which had a bad effect on some of us, and me in particular. I was having a lot of laughs until the Christmas carols came on and then I suddenly felt a lump in my throat and missed my family so much. We had worked so hard for so long and felt quite good about all that had been achieved, but homesickness was becoming more frequent and we were really burnt out. I knew that while I would miss all the activity and excitement of working in an emergency setting, the time was coming very soon when I just had to get home to be with my family again. However, Dale, my pilot friend, had other ideas.

AJIEP RE-VISITED

Mike and I were gradually handing over to our replacements as we neared completion of our contracts. As both people taking over from us had been working in Kenya and Sudan for some time, they were fairly up to date on all that was happening. Stepping back, however, was not as easy as it sounds, as we both wanted to still be involved, and the knowledge that someone else would soon be doing my job left me feeling a bit strange. I had the problem of wanting to go home and at the same time feeling that I wanted to stay and keep on at the job.

Once again, it was a case of the guy on the right shoulder saying one thing, and the guy on the left shoulder saying the opposite.

I had been in this situation before and knew that this was not as strange as it sounds. It was my last weekend in Loki and because of the handover I was not under the same pressure as I had been for months. Mike told me that there was a rotation going to Ajiep on the Sunday and enquired if I would like to go on it and see Ajiep from the ground rather than the air. It would also give me a chance to say goodbye to the people based there. I was thrilled to have the opportunity and asked Mike to go with me, but Dale was flying so Mike said no thanks! He had never overcome his fear of flying with Dale.

We headed off on Sunday morning and Dale was in fine form. He remarked that the last time we had gone to Ajiep together it had been a lot colder in the plane, with no doors. He asked what my plans were for the future and I informed him that I just wanted to get home to my family and was not looking beyond that. He then shocked me by asking if I would be interested in coming back after Christmas and working for him in Loki. He was arranging a contract to fly goods into Uganda and wanted me to look after the logistics. He told me that I would be well paid, but when I asked what he was up to he just smiled. As much as I liked the idea of working with him, I declined the offer.

The plane we were flying in was the Antonov that we had made the airdrop from and it was loaded with supplies. I was sitting on a fold-down seat immediately behind Dale as we came in to land and as we hit the airstrip with a bump and continued towards the end of the strip I heard Dale swear at the top of his voice. He hit the brakes so hard that I was pushed hard into my seat belt. I thought that the plane would go over onto its nose, but it settled back down as it stopped. Dale was ranting and pointing at the ground in front of us. Someone had dug a small trench across the airstrip, and we could see an electrical cable at the bottom of the trench. When we checked later we discovered that the people doing the work had thought that the rotation was arriving the next day and that it was therefore safe enough to cut a trench three-quarters of the way down the airstrip! I could see the funny side of being stuck in Sudan on the last rotation before I was to head home and Dale eventually started to laugh too. The take-off, however, was going to have to be done on an airstrip that was shorter than normal, but once Dale had got over his annoyance, he said that we were not to worry, as the length available to us was sufficient. I, however, wondered if this was another of Dale's 'experiments.'

While the supplies were being offloaded one of the nurses brought me on a guided tour of the Ajiep camp. They had certainly had a tough time on the ground. I was shown where part of the camp had been flooded and was in awe of the tenacity of the team, which had overcome very difficult conditions. Ordinary people in an extraordinary situation had achieved so much against the odds. One girl, aged about ten, walked beside me holding my hand and the nurse told me that the girl had been at death's door and it was a miracle that she had pulled through.

She was literally skin and bones, like a stick person in an LS Lowry painting, but was all smiles. When I returned home to Ireland, I saw the same child on the BBC documentary about Sudan and was shocked at the condition that she had been in just a month prior to my visit.

I visited the hospital tent where people with various ailments were being treated and was introduced to the local staff and the patients. An old man was standing at the top end of the tent and as he looked at me, he spoke to a member of our local staff called Alpha Kilo (I didn't know his actual name) and the two then approached me. The old man held out his hand, spoke in Dinka and shook hands with me. There were tears in his eyes. I asked Alpha Kilo what was being said and he told me that the old man wanted to know who I was. He had informed him that I was the person who arranged for the supplies to be sent to Ajiep and the man had just said, 'Thank you for giving me back my life.'

I felt humbled and explained that I was just part of a team and it was the teamwork that made it all possible, but it was nice to see what the result of all that work had been on the ground.

A few people travelled back from Ajiep to Loki with us and they were excited because they were going on R&R. It was soon time for take-off and Dale told us not to worry, but to be aware that it would be quite abrupt, due to the reduced length of the airstrip. He did his impression of his fighter-jet take-off and we lifted well before the trench, safe as usual, but left asking ourselves, 'What if …?'

We landed back at Loki and Mike wanted to know how it was in Ajiep. 'Full of the most unlikely heroes you will ever come across,' was my reply.

It was time to party and say goodbye. Bottles of beer were bought in Kate Camp and we had a great night. We were both elated at the thought of going home and still a little sad.

We were due to leave Loki the next morning and spend most of the following week in Nairobi. I knew that I needed a bit of time to relax before I headed home. I remembered what had happened to me after Bosnia and the effect of going from one lifestyle to another in a matter of hours was really unsettling. It was far better to unwind in Nairobi before travelling. I would be back in Ireland exactly a week before Christmas and felt that it would be diffi-cult enough to adjust. I was going to miss Mike; we had been through so much together. And so we left Loki as we had arrived – together. I shed a tear as I climbed up into the plane – I was missing it already. No more 47-degree heat, no more Dale and his mad escapades, and no more stress. It was now someone else's problem, but it had been an experience I would never forget. The poem I wrote after returning home hopefully tells its own story:

Victims
Sometimes a smell
Or sound or scene
Brings me back
To places I have been,
I see puzzled faces
Of old and young
As they wonder
Why me?
What have I done wrong?

DUBLIN

A week later I arrived back in Dublin airport around mid-morning, having flown overnight from Nairobi to London and then onwards to Dublin. I was met at the airport by Liz and David. I was so happy to be back and felt so different from when I had returned from Bosnia, a year earlier. I felt that this time I had performed much better and was very satisfied with what had been achieved. Life had changed a lot in twelve months.

Bosnia: Bullet and shell damage plus landmines near Sarajevo Airport

Bosnia: please keep off the grass

Bosnia: Ray's apartment in Sarajevo; note damage to ground floor level windows and path outside

Bosnia: Sarajevo Airport car park

Bosnia: Mine action centre in Sarajevo, they were kept busy!

Bosnia: overgrown garden in Sarajevo due to landmines

South Sudan: my tent in a scenic setting in Nyamylel

South Sudan: Ray outside the clinic in Nyamylel

Loki, Kenya: Dale eating out

South Sudan: a barely alive Perdi and his father

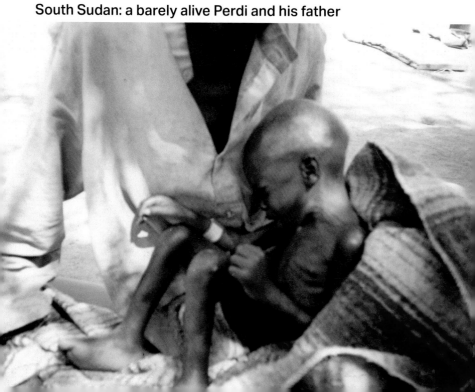

South Sudan: Ray and bodyguard (note rifle over bodyguard's shoulder)

Loki, Kenya: Mike and Ray on the day it rained in Loki

Loki: the Antonov aircraft used at Ajiep with the loading doors still on the aircraft

Somewhere over South Sudan: The Antonov without doors and after the Ajiep airdrop

Sierra Leone: Beth's Clinic, Freetown

Sierra Leone: Prosthetic limbs being manufactured at Murraytown camp

Sierra Leone: Some of the thousands of occupants at Approved School Camp, in Freetown

Sierra Leone: a very distressed Moses at Lakka UAC camp, Freetown (photo courtesy of Kim Houghton)

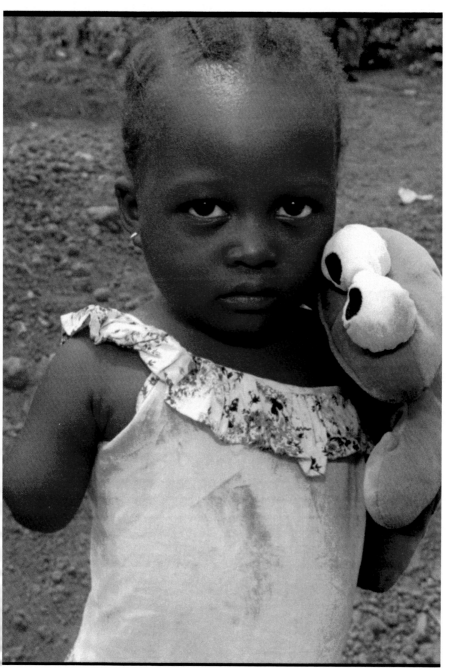
Sierra Leone: "Lucy" and the ever-present Cookie monster (photo courtesy of Kim Houghton)

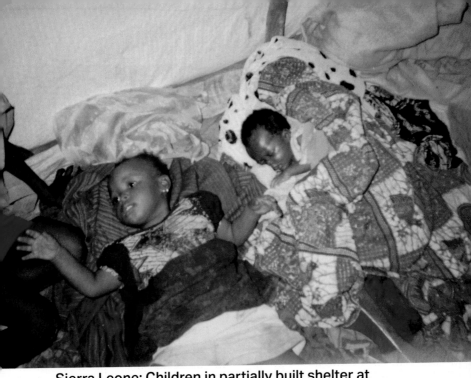

Sierra Leone: Children in partially built shelter at
Approved School Camp, Freetown

Mozambique: Engineer "Michael" and one of the drivers in
Beira

Mozambique: Engineer "Peter" and Ray at Muchinessa school at an early stage of construction

Mozambique: Engineer "Peter" at Muchinessa school in the later stages of construction

Mozambique: The team hard at work in Buzi

Mozambique: "Chica" the pet monkey's first week in Buzi

Mozambique: the Fastank in Bueni solved the water problems on site

Mozambique: Work completed – Mairead and Ray on the river Buzi for the last time

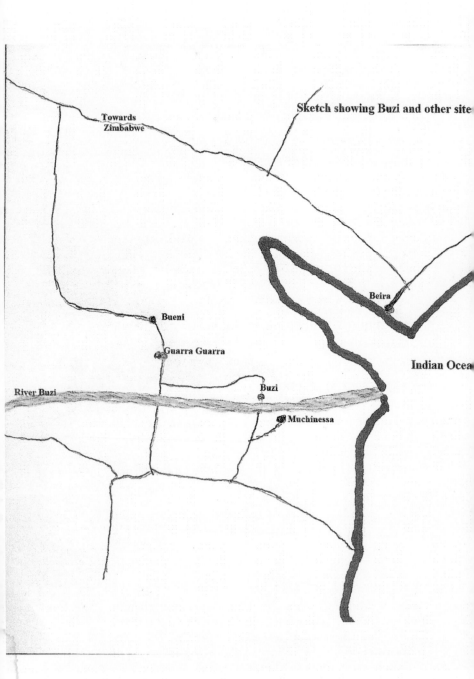

Mozambique: sketch showing the different locations
involved around Buzi

5

Sierra Leone, West Africa

DEBRIEF

The last year of the millennium dawned and I went for my post-contract medical check-up. I was weighed at the clinic and various samples were taken. I felt fit and was looking forward to my debriefing with Concern in Dublin. Life was good. If I could have foreseen how I would be before the year ended, I would not have been so cocky.

Mike had travelled up from Cork and was also having his medical and debrief. We went out to lunch together with our wives. We laughed and joked, bored our wives, I'm sure, and then headed into the Concern office for separate meetings. We were encouraged to give honest feedback to HR, and this I did.

'Tell it as it is,' has always been my motto – sometimes it upsets people, but it is better to be straight. I detest people telling me what I want to hear.

After a while I was asked if I would like to work for Concern again in the future. I replied that I would. I was told that there was an emergency situation in Sierra Leone, West Africa and that my services as a construction supervisor would be required. I was not needed immediately, as there was a person in place at the time but would be required in a few months' time. This suited me perfectly.

NEW BRIEFING

I was updated about the situation in Sierra Leone and realised that it was very serious. Most of the country had been overrun by rebels, the Revolutionary United Front (RUF), and the atrocities carried out by this group were shocking. Hacking, which involved cutting off hands or feet, or both, with machetes, was common-place and the population was in a state of terror. Thousands had fled from the countryside into Freetown, the capital. Large areas of the country were at this stage under the control of the RUF and Freetown had been attacked and large numbers of civilians killed. Boy soldiers had been 'recruited' by the RUF and most, if not all, were on drugs. I was shown photographs of amputees – some as young as three years old – as well as victims of gunshot and shrapnel wounds and warned that the atrocities were the worst ever witnessed by experienced aid workers. Concern was not pulling any punches.

A photographer from the *Irish Times* who had been to Freetown held a photographic exhibition in Dublin that clearly showed some of the victims and the circumstances in which they were living. One photograph showed two families living in the maintenance pit of a commercial garage. Thousands were living out of doors at a large football stadium or sheltering under trees, or anywhere else that they could find shelter from the blistering sun and tropical storms. It was estimated that up to four hundred thousand people had been displaced. The normal coping mecha-nism in this sort of situation is for people to move in with family or friends, but the numbers of displaced people were so great that this solution was impossible. Many houses in Freetown had been destroyed, but it was considered safer to be in a city than out in the countryside, where there was absolutely no protection. The IDPs desperately needed help and Concern was responding, along with a lot of other NGOs. This was a real emergency and I very much wanted to be part of the humanitarian response.

TRAINING COURSES

It looked like I might be spending some time in Guinea as well as in Sierra Leone, so I put my name down with APSO for a spoken French course, as well as some other courses. I made good use of the library in APSO and started researching the situation. The official language in Sierra Leone was English, while in Guinea I would need French. I was back in training mode and felt very motivated. I found that going into APSO gave me a focus, as well as giving me the opportunity to meet like-minded people. I kept busy and almost before I knew it, the time for departure had arrived. However, my family situation had changed drastically in just a few months.

FAMILY MATTERS

My mother had had a stroke in 1996 and was confined to a wheel-chair. She had been a very fit and active woman all her life and not being able to get about under her own steam now was extremely hard for her. While I was preparing for Sierra Leone her health deteriorated further and she was admitted to hospital again, where she had yet another stroke. She was in a coma and not aware of her surroundings. The situation was bleak and all we could do was wait for the inevitable. I knew that my mother's time on this earth was coming to a close.

Concern had by this time applied for a visa for me to travel to Guinea en route to Sierra Leone, and this was valid for only a limited amount of time. I went into Concern's office and explained my personal situation and asked if they could find someone else to take my place for Sierra Leone. There was no one else available, so I told Concern that I wanted to delay my departure for the time being. Shortly after my meeting with Concern my mother passed away. It was a tough time. Concern had suggested in an earlier meeting with them that a visit to a counsellor would be required prior to going to Sierra Leone as well as after returning home.

They felt this was necessary due to what I would be witnessing while working with victims of the war.

I visited the counsellor and told her of my recent experiences, both overseas and at home. I was worried she might feel that, due to my recent bereavement, I was not a suitable candidate but I stated honestly that for my own peace of mind I needed to get moving. Sitting at home was not going to help me or anyone else. I could imagine my mother saying, 'You have put your hand to the plough, now there is no turning back.'

When I had discussed the situation with my father his answer had been, 'You can help someone there, staying here won't change the situation, go where you are needed most.'

I was relieved. I advised Concern that I was ready to travel and a week after my mother's funeral, I was on my way to Africa again.

DEPARTURE

Liz drove me to the airport and we had a tearful farewell. It seemed to get harder to leave each time. However, once I was on the plane, I became focused on what lay ahead. My first stop was Paris and from there I would get a flight on to Conakry in Guinea. The plan was to overnight in Conakry and then be flown by helicopter into Sierra Leone the next day. Everything had been organised by Concern in advance, so it should have been plain sailing. 'Men make plans and the gods laugh.'

CONAKRY, GUINEA, WEST AFRICA

About an hour before we were due to land in Conakry I casually looked through my passport and suddenly realised that the visa for entry into Guinea had expired the previous day. With all that had been going on at home the expiry date had been overlooked, both by me and by Concern. The plane landed and within seconds of disembarking I was covered in sweat due to the heat and high humidity. We were directed to passport control. I decided to bluff my way and just hand in the passport and hope no one noticed the date on the visa. No such luck, however. The visa was checked and I was informed in French that it had expired. I was already putting my French lessons to practical use. I explained as best I could about the reason for my delay. The officer was sympathetic, but this did not alter the fact that I didn't have a valid entry visa. I knew that they would be within their rights to put me on the plane and send me back to Paris. But I decided to take a gamble and so stuck a twenty-dollar note into the passport and asked the officer to check the passport again. The twenty-dollar note vanished and I was upgraded immediately from illegal visitor to VIP. Orders were barked out and a porter told to take my bags and help me out to a taxi. Concern had booked me a room in the hotel in Conakry where the logistics unit for the UN were based.

The international airport at Lungi in Freetown was not operational due to the security situation, so the only way to reach Sierra Leone from Guinea was by UN helicopter. My instructions were to go to the UN office and let them know that I had arrived and was ready to travel on the next day. There were two UN logisticians, one Danish and the other English. They seemed quite stressed and told me that communications with Sierra Leone were very difficult. They informed me that they had no booking for me, had never heard of me and that I could be waiting for up to a week before they moved me on. Their tone clearly indicated that arguing the situation was not a good idea. A softly-softly approach was required. I thanked them for letting me know and replied that I would arrange an official request for my flight. I asked if they would be free to meet me for a drink in the hotel later to give me some updates on the situation across the border. This seemed to calm the situation down. I tried to phone Concern in Sierra Leone, but the telephone lines were not working so decided to try again in the morning.

When I met the UN guys for a drink later they informed me that lots of people were passing through Guinea on their way to Sierra Leone and that they were under constant pressure. I told them that I would wait patiently and read a book until they could find a slot for me, however long that took. I think they were a bit surprised by my laissez-faire approach and we parted on friendly terms that night. Next morning I tried to get in touch with Concern in Sierra Leone but again could not make contact, so I telephoned Concern Dublin and told them that I was topping up my suntan in Guinea, and they agreed to let the Concern office in Sierra Leone know that I was safe. It looked like I was going to have a few days of downtime, sitting in Guinea. I decided to leave the UN logs guys alone during the day and saw them again at dinner that night, when they told me that they were trying to get me on a flight. I took it easy the next day and in the afternoon one of them approached me and said that he had found a slot for the following day. I let Concern in Dublin know the situation. I was aware that I had used the old Mike Lima approach in dealing with the problem – be polite and thank people for their efforts and this will, in most cases, get you much further than shouting and being aggressive.

HELICOPTER TO FREETOWN

Early next morning I was ready to go and along with several other people was picked up by UN transport. When we arrived at the airport a UN official asked for our passports. I asked to speak to him away from the group and told him about the visa issue.

'Right, thanks for telling me, I'll sort it,' he said. The passports were checked by a local official, but mine was not queried. I breathed a sigh of relief. The helicopter that we boarded was a Russian-manufactured troop carrier, a very basic aircraft, and we sat on two benches facing one another, with our luggage stacked in front of us. The pilot explained that for security reasons we would fly out over the sea and that as we approached Freetown we would come in very low and fast. This was because the RUF had rocket-propelled grenades (RPGs) and by using this method of approach we would be less of a target. When we landed we were to grab our luggage, disembark quickly and stay away from the back of the chopper due to the low rotor, which would still be spinning. The rear rotors on helicopters spin vertically and are quite low, so if you want to avoid losing your head, you stay away from the back! I knew about staying away from the rear end as this had been part of the Red R training that I had undergone in the UK, but it still felt good to know what was required.

The chopper was to be on the ground for just a few minutes, which was the SOP for insecure locations. Despite the security issues I enjoyed the journey over the sea – the sense of speed from flying so low was exhilarating and I was certainly getting a buzz. As soon as the wheels touched the ground we disembarked and within minutes the new passengers were on board and the chopper took off. Welcome to Sierra Leone.

First day in Freetown

A woman came up to me at the helipad and introduced herself as Toireas, the country director for Concern in Sierra Leone. The Concern hat that she was wearing made identification easy and we were driven to the Concern house, which was quite a short distance away from the helipad. I was shown my room and intro-duced to the cook, who was a middle-aged man.

First things first, however – the security briefing. Toireas explained that we were in an area of Freetown called Aberdeen. A lot of places in Sierra Leone have English or Scottish names. Aberdeen is located along a peninsula, which made us a bit more secure. There were two roads leading to that part of the penin-sula and both had roadblocks with constant military cover. The house was in a walled compound overlooking the sea, but more importantly, it was less than 100 metres' walking distance from a helipad. Various locations had been designated by the UN as evacuation points and the Concern house was one. There was a beach close by called Lumley, a beautiful place with several miles of white sand. I could see straight away that I was going to like the place, especially after my time in Kenya and Sudan.

The security situation, however, was very unstable. The front line was about 23 miles away from us and there had already been attacks by the RUF, right into Freetown. Security was provided mainly by troops from Nigeria, who were part of a military alliance called ECOMOG. The Sierra Leonean army alone had not been able to repel the RUF and were at that stage being re-formed and re-trained with assistance from the British. Added to this mix were mercenaries and local militias, so it was a real hot spot of activity.

There was a curfew from 1800 hours until 0700 hours, during which no one was allowed on the road. The staff had to leave in plenty of time to get home and in the same way, they could not travel to work before 0700 hours. Although I had been made aware of a lot of the restrictions before I left Dublin, now that I was in country the situation was much bleaker than I had anticipated. Clearly, it was a highly dangerous place!

Our official working week was Monday to Friday and a half day Saturday. Right, I thought, I will just have to work within the limitations and be really focused. The good news was that while Toireas was giving me all the information, sandwiches and tea had been prepared by the cook and I quickly demolished them. More sandwiches were brought and the briefing continued. I was enjoying the set-up already – tea, sandwiches and a beautiful beach across the road and all the time I was getting more information. Toireas informed me that after lunch we would go to the office, meet the staff, and she would give me more details about the work that Concern were doing.

Well-fed and watered, we headed for the office. A short distance from the house we were stopped at a roadblock. This consisted of a wall of sandbags laid diagonally across most of the road, with a small opening on one side for traffic to pass through. A second row of sandbags was laid a short distance beyond the first, with the opening for traffic on the opposite side of the road. Near the edge of the road, under a tree, was an observation post manned by a soldier with a machine gun and we had to stop and identify ourselves to the troops. As this was the main road from our house to the office, most of the troops were familiar with the car because it had Concern logos on the doors and across the bonnet. I was introduced as the new person working for Concern and we were instructed to drive on slowly. We meandered around the roadblock and headed into the office.

Mr Ray Would Like a Monkey

THE OFFICE

The office was a single-storey building situated at the end of a narrow road with large drainage ditches on both sides. I was introduced to the local office staff, which consisted of a bookkeeper, an admin/HR officer and a young logistician named James. The rest of the local staff consisted of an engineer, a nurse and dozens of labourers and carpenters. I was told that there were only two other international staff – Catherine, an accountant from Ireland and Beth, a nurse from Canada. It was not a large set-up in terms of international personnel, but as it turned out there was a huge amount of work in progress. There was one large open area in the office where the local staff worked, and two other smaller rooms. Beth and Toireas worked in one office and I was to share an office with the accountant, who was away at that time carrying out some work in Liberia.

I got settled in, read the handover notes from my predecessor and then headed for the toilet. All the tea was running though me. I smelled the toilet before I saw it. Memories of Bosnia and the lack of water to flush the toilet came back to me. I enquired if there was a water shortage at the office and was told that there was water, but that they were waiting for a plumber to fix the toilet as it would not flush. Unfortunately, it seemed that it was exceedingly difficult to get a plumber. Civil war creates unforeseen difficulties and it seemed that one of these was a shortage of plumbers. Before I had left Ireland Liz had bought me a Leatherman tool, similar to a Swiss Army knife. It had all sorts of blades, screwdrivers and cutting implements and opened out to form a pliers, just what the doctor ordered for quick repairs. I took the cover off the WC cistern and could see straight away what the problem was. The screw holding the handle to the flushing system had come loose and the handle was rotating freely. A few turns of the screwdriver part of the Leatherman tool fixed the problem, and the toilet flushed perfectly when I pressed the handle. I informed Edna, the admin officer, that the plumber was not required and was greeted with a thank you and a big smile.

How to win friends and influence people – fix the toilet on your first day.

Toireas talked me though the handover notes and let me know that she was available to help me in any way she could. She explained what was happening in and around Freetown, and the limitations, in a very clear manner. I was impressed. I knew that she had to be terribly busy because of all that was going on, but she was calm and took all the time necessary to answer all my questions. We agreed that the next day we should visit the various sites together, where she would introduce me to the engineer and various foremen. This would give me an initial introduction and then I would re-visit the sites when I could get detailed information, at my own pace. It was made clear that I was to be in charge of construction, but any support that I needed would be made available. She warned me that one of the sites, situated close by in a place called Murraytown, consisted of a camp for amputees and their families and that several previous visitors had been very distressed by what they had seen. I appreciated the warning but already knew from the photographs that I had seen in Dublin that Murraytown Camp would be stressful for me, too.

As the working day ended, Beth, the Canadian nurse, returned to the office and I had a chat with her. My first impression was of a quietly spoken, reserved person. She oversaw the Concern health programme and was based in the grounds of an educational facility that was known as Approved School. There were thousands of IDPs there and Concern was busy constructing emergency shelter. Beth outlined some of the issues at Approved School and I was told that it would be one of the sites that we would be visiting the following day. I wasn't in the country a day and I was beginning to feel that the amount of work involved was enormous. The workload for Sudan had been huge but we had a large number of international and local staff there. The situation in Sierra Leone was very different, in that we had a very small team, so I could see that I would need to plan my work carefully if I was not to be overwhelmed.

Due to the curfew, every minute was precious so a decision had been made to employ local people for housekeeping duties. There was literally no time for shopping, for food, or for cooking, as every minute was accounted for during the day and a lot more work was done at night-time when we were stuck in the house. We left the office that evening and headed through the road-blocks back to the house, where a nice meal awaited us. It was very warm, even at night-time and the sweat rolled off me. It had been very warm in Sudan and I had adjusted well while there, but in Sierra Leone the high humidity made the place feel like an oven. I had the windows open in my bedroom, with just the mosquito wire netting and a mosquito net draped over my bed to protect me from the malaria-carrying mosquitoes. It was for good reason that Sierra Leone was also known as the 'white man's grave'. Sometimes wire mesh and netting is just not enough.

SITE VISITS

I was up early the next day, had a shower and was looking forward to my first full day on the job. Within minutes my clean shirt was stuck to my back. I had noticed that the wardrobe in my bedroom had a cable running through it with electric bulbs attached. When I enquired over breakfast about this strange arrangement, I was informed that the bulbs were there to stop my clothes becoming damp and mouldy due to the high humidity.

After breakfast Toireas drove Beth and me into the office. Beth then headed off to Approved School and our local driver brought Toireas and me out to the first site, Murraytown. I was shocked and appalled at what I saw. There were dozens of people there missing arms or legs, or sometimes both. They were the victims of gunshot wounds or 'chopping.' Chopping involved cutting off hands or feet with machetes and was the RUF's preferred method for terrorising the population. Some victims had had both hands cut off. The youngest was a little girl who was about three years old. It was a terrible sight and I felt sickened. Men, women and children, no one had been spared. I took a deep breath and thought that I just had to get on with the job. Otherwise I would not be able to cope.

The camp had been part of a football pitch that was located alongside a health clinic and there were some other unidentified buildings in a dilapidated state. A large temporary structure had been erected using heavy plastic sheeting and dozens of people were living inside it. Some latrines had been dug, but a lot more were required. Another building on-site had been identified as available for conversion to living accommodation but needed a lot of work, as part of the roof was missing. Cooking areas or 'kitchens' were required where the able-bodied could prepare meals on fires, and they also needed to provide some shelter from tropical storms. There was a water supply nearby, but it needed to be extended. A building programme to construct new temporary houses using bush sticks and plastic sheeting was about to start, but needed setting out to get the best use from the space available. Bush sticks were like normal tree branches, but they grew straight out of the ground – we needed thousands of them.

An organisation called Handicap International was on-site, working in a tiny building where they were measuring people for prosthetic limbs, manufacturing the limbs and then fitting them to the amputees. They needed a bigger building for this work, as well as some space for rehabilitation services to teach the amputees how to use their new prosthetic limbs. Electric power was an issue, so they had a generator on-site.

I was informed of all of this in the first twenty minutes! The message was clear – this is what we need, and we need it as soon as possible.

My plan was to visit each site and get the basic information from those working there to make the most out of my limited day. It would have been quite easy to get sucked into the problems of the first site, but I knew that approach would be a mistake. I informed the Murraytown foreman of my plans and promised to return the next day when we could get down to specifics. Next we moved on to Approved School, where Beth was based. Toireas pointed out the tiny clinic where the health programme was being implemented and it was clearly far too small for the work involved. There were lots of people queuing up outside waiting to be seen. There had been another building nearby, but it had been blown up and all that remained were the floor slab and foundations. This site was quite large and split into four sections. In each section the building work involved providing shelter, kitchens, latrines and a water supply. Plastic sheeting and bush sticks were in high demand, as we had to house at least four thousand people on this one site alone. Because of the high flooding risk from tropical storms, large drainage ditches were being dug around each section and pedestrian bridges needed to be constructed to allow access from one section to another. The site was so big that we had several section foremen, as well as a site engineer. The engineer wanted decisions made on various issues as soon as possible and seemed to be glad that he had someone with whom to share his technical problems again. I tried to absorb the basic information and then, again, like in Murraytown, told the engineer that I would be back soon. I visited a few more places and the day flew by. By the time I returned to the office I had an overall impression of what was going on but needed to get down to specifics.

There was another site 21 miles away, out in a place called Waterloo, which I had yet to visit. Toireas told me that to get to Waterloo we had to pass through over 40 roadblocks and the site was almost on the front line, so it would have to be inspected on a separate day. It was clear to me already that unless I had a very structured approach, a lot of time could be lost. Since my predecessor had left a few weeks earlier the workload had increased enormously, with the result that the local engineer and foremen were becoming overwhelmed. Because more and more people were pouring into Freetown every day, the demands being made on all the NGOs were accelerating. It was time to update the plans to accommodate all the new demands.

I returned to the office exhausted and with a pounding headache. I told Toireas that I would be happy to go out with a driver on my own the following day and start to address some of the issues. I was glad to get back to the house that night and to have the time to think about what I needed to do. We had an unwritten rule that drinking alcohol was restricted to a minimum during the week, as it was too easy to slip into bad habits, what with being locked down each night at 1800 hours. After my first visit to Murraytown I could see that the rule made a lot of sense. I went to bed exhausted and had terrible nightmares that involved people with no hands gathering around me and asking for help. I had an unsettled night tossing and turning, but when I woke up the next morning I was itching to get to work. There was just so much to do.

SECOND VISIT TO CAMPS

I had only a driver for company for my second visit to the camps, so I was basically on my own in terms of decision-making. My initial approach to the staff on-site was to ask them what their problems were and to inform them that I was there to assist them. Most people are reluctant at first to go down this road, as they are unsure of a new person on the job. Will their admission of needing help be interpreted as a sign of weakness that could be used against them? I tried to win their confidence by asking them not only to indicate the problems, but also to let me know what they thought the solutions to the problems might be. I felt that they were testing me and that I had to win their confidence. Respect can only be earned, not demanded.

My first port of call was Murraytown, as it was nearest to the office. There were many issues that needed sorting and, where possible, decisions were made immediately. Sketches were prepared quickly, materials lists drawn up and supply request forms approved by me. The system was that the engineer had authority to prepare the request for supplies, but only a senior member of the team could actually authorise the purchase of goods. Concern operated a very strict financial control system, but nevertheless moved rapidly. By lunchtime we had moved across town to Approved School, where the same process was repeated. Again, decisions that could be made immediately were

Mr Ray Would Like a Monkey

acted upon. There were of course lots of issues that needed following up and these had to be discussed back at the office, but in the main the technical decisions were all mine and I was free to get on with work that had previously been approved and for which finance was available. Making decisions on large-scale new work was a different story, as I had to have approval for spending money on any new projects.

I was looking forward to my first weekend, when I could sit back and take time to think – it seemed that everything was happening at a hundred miles an hour. When I got back to the office I found that visitors from Ireland had arrived, a man and a woman – a newspaper journalist and a photographer. They were going to stay with us for a few days and visit some of the places where we were working, to write an article for an Irish newspaper.

THE VISITORS

It was nice to have the journalist and photographer staying with us, as it gave us someone else to talk to at night-time. They asked if they could start by travelling with me to the various camps the next day. I was quite happy to have them along, but was a bit concerned at how they would react when they saw the situation on the ground. I was particularly concerned about bringing them to the amputee camp at Murraytown and tried to prepare them for the nightmare scenario. They asked lots of intelligent questions and I was glad to fill them in. Despite that, I could see the horror on their faces immediately as we disembarked from the car next morning at Murraytown Camp. The photographer, Kim, was a young woman and I was worried that she would be very upset, but she just kept clicking away with the camera, although she was noticeably pale. I admired her professionalism. The journalist, Conor, was visibly shaken, but again was a true professional. It was reassuring to be with such people. Conor wanted to know all the details about the size of the camp, the number of people involved, where they cooked their food, where they got water and so on. I thought that he would be a great asset for planning, as he was asking all the right questions, and this is what you need to be doing when you are dealing with a new situation. I explained to Conor that the situation that we found ourselves in necessitated a high level of cooperation with other NGOs and the UN. We all had to pull together.

In Murraytown, the timber for framing the houses was supplied and erected by the Concern construction team, the plastic sheeting was supplied by the UN and fitted by Concern, the water supply was installed by Oxfam, and finally Handicap International measured, manufactured, and fitted prosthetic limbs. In addition, the sanitation needs were met by Concern by building latrines in various locations. We were not providing food, as the government was looking after this part of the jigsaw, but the residents needed somewhere to cook and so we had to build 'kitchens'. These consisted of rectangular enclosures placed at each corner of the site. They were constructed from a timber frame with the side walls and roofs finished with corrugated iron sheets for protection from the rain and wind. Most of the cooking was done by the able-bodied residents using small fires, although we experimented with clay-built ovens as well.

It was this type of set-up that we had to repeat in all the other camps, as the basic needs of the residents, wherever they were, were shelter, sanitation, food and water. By the time Conor and Kim had visited several of the sites I felt that they were sadder and wiser, as well as exhausted. My head was buzzing with all that had to be done, but at the same time I felt that I was making some progress – but was it enough? Only time would tell.

ATTACK AT SONGO

We normally stopped work on Saturday around lunchtime. News, however, had come in about an attack by the RUF on a small village called Songo, which was out near Waterloo, and the journalists were interested in seeing the place. We checked with the UN to see if we could visit and were informed that it was possible, but to be very careful. We drove out towards the village and went through numerous roadblocks. I was a bit concerned that we were getting too close to the front line and so we checked with the soldiers on the roadblocks close to the village. They informed us that the RUF had retreated and that ECOMOG had troops in the area.

This information didn't particularly reassure me, as it was just as easy to be shot by friendly fire as by the RUF, so we travelled slowly and carefully. We eventually arrived at another roadblock, which consisted of barrels in the road with timber across the top of the barrels. On top of one of the barrels was a human skull. That got my attention!

The soldiers approached and asked where we were going. We explained about the Irish journalists, that they wanted to take photographs, and enquired if this was permissible.

You just never know how troops will react to cameras, particularly in a volatile area. They gave us permission and mentioned that there were some dead RUF people nearby. A short distance down the road we turned onto a dirt track road. We had only travelled a few hundred metres when we saw two bodies on the side of the track. We stopped the car, got out, and Kim started taking photographs. I suggested that we should only stay a few minutes and felt that the place was far too dangerous, as the RUF could be nearby. The bodies were bloated, stank to high heaven and one of them had been decapitated. Conor was standing behind Kim and when she stepped back away from the first body Conor stepped back as well, but in doing so, stepped onto the second body. He jumped away from the corpse and looked like he was going to be sick. When he got back into the car he didn't look the best for the experience.

We then travelled on into the village. It had been shot up and we could see clearly where bullets had gone through the walls of the dwellings. There were no residents to be seen and there was an eerie feeling about. As we neared the end of the village we came across yet another ECOMOG patrol. One of the soldiers started to complain about the camera and it was obvious to us that he was drunk. He kept saying that he did not want his photo taken. We told him that there was no problem and that we would move on. However, when we tried to move away he became argumentative and insisted that we take his photo. I was glad of the training that I had received during my Red R course when the Royal Engineers had advised me on how to deal with such a situation – stay calm and don't do anything to make the situation worse.

The soldier's photo was taken and he then seemed happy enough, but it was clear that we needed to remove ourselves from the location without delay. We made our way out of the village and headed back towards Freetown. When we eventually reached our house at Lumley I was tired and hungry and felt that what we had done had probably not been the smartest move, although I appreciated that a journalist has to get close to the action. We sat down for the evening meal, but Conor hadn't been feeling well and didn't appear at the table. It is very easy in Sierra Leone for people to suddenly become sickly, especially foreigners, but the sight of the two bodies and the smell would have been enough to put most people off their food. I tried to put the experience behind me and had my dinner.

A BEAUTIFUL SUNDAY MORNING

I woke up early the next morning and looked out my window at a beautiful blue sky. It looked so nice that I decided to have a swim before breakfast. No one else in the house was up and so shortly after 0800 hours I unlocked the back door, walked by the security guard and out of the compound. I strolled the short distance to the Lumley road, crossed the road and walked towards the sea.

'Beautiful,' I thought, and started to walk along the beach.

Suddenly the peaceful setting was shattered. There was shouting, with soldiers running up the road and across the beach towards me.

'Hands up, hands up,' they shouted and pointed their rifles at me.

I stopped dead in my tracks and asked what was up. For a second I thought that maybe there was a problem with landmines.

Mr Ray Would Like a Monkey

The soldiers continued to shout at me even though I now had my hands as high as they could go.

'Don't shoot, I'm Irish,' I pleaded.

Even as I said it, I thought how stupid it sounded, but it was the only thing that I could think of. They stopped shouting and I asked them what the problem was.

'You are on the beach,' one soldier shouted.

'I know that, but what is the problem?' I asked again.

'You are not allowed on this beach,' he replied. 'The RUF attacked from the sea before so no one is allowed on the beach.'

I was starting to get a bit annoyed and at the same time realised that they were very jumpy. I told him that I was sorry but had not seen any sign saying that the beach was out of bounds. He agreed that there was no sign but even so, I could have been shot. I explained that I had only arrived recently in Freetown, wasn't aware of the no-go area and apologised again. We all calmed down a bit after that and when I told him that I was working for Concern, he seemed satisfied and we all left the beach together. You don't have to do something stupid to get shot in a war zone, just going for a swim could do it. I went back to the house and had my breakfast, but I was a bit shook up. What next? I thought, the place was just full of surprises.

LAKKA

The journalists were very keen to meet different people and hear their stories and there were a lot of people around who had horrific tales to tell. There was an Irish priest called Father Jude in Freetown. He ran a teacher training college located a few miles from the village of Lakka. He had heard about the newspaper people and thought that they might like to meet some of the young victims who had been abducted by the RUF, but who had escaped and were now in a rehabilitation unit situated beside the beach. There was also a large number of unaccompanied children (known as UACs) in the unit who had lost contact with their families. When a village was attacked, people ran in every direction and it was not unusual for children to become separated from their parents, with the result that there were groups of children who did not know if their parents were alive or dead or where they were. This situation had a terribly traumatic effect on them. Not only had they been terrified by the attacks, but they lacked the reassurance of having their parents with them. Some of these children were incredibly young and it was heart-breaking to see them. The building they were located in had originally been a hostel for French holidaymakers, but the only French people in Freetown at this stage were aid workers.

We met Father Jude near the training college and travelled out to Lakka. There were many children, ranging in age from about four years old up to about sixteen, boys and girls. Some of the boys had been boy soldiers and there were young girls who had been taken away as 'wives' for the RUF. All were quite traumatised and efforts were being made to rehabilitate them by providing counselling. As soon as I got out of the car a young boy, aged around nine or ten, came up to me, held my hand and leaned in against me. The child smelled like he hadn't had a wash for weeks and Jude told me that the boy, whom they called Moses, was terrified of water and also that he could not or would not speak. He looked so sad that my heart went out to him and I felt terribly angry that anyone could have treated a child so badly that he was now in such terrible psychological distress. He was pitiful. I had not been aware that my feelings about the situation were so obvious, but as Kim started to take photographs she commented, 'I see that you are not made of stone after all.' I replied that if I could get my hands on the people responsible for ill-treating the children, I would want to kill them – not the conduct associated with an aid worker, I knew, but nevertheless that was how I felt.

We were invited into the building to sit in on some of the debriefings that were taking place.

The first interview was with a boy who had been taken from his family, drugged and trained to kill. He looked like he was about twelve years old. The counsellor talked him through a series of questions and there was initially a certain air of bravado about him. He was not sure how many people he had killed and gave the impression that he couldn't care less. However, as the interview continued he started to unravel, became less cocky, and eventually ended up in tears, just like a normal twelve-year-old who has been caught doing something that he shouldn't have. It was heart-breaking to watch.

The next lad was around the same age as the first boy and had a similar story to tell. He had been taken from his family at gunpoint by the rebels. The rebels had told the mothers left in his village to bring their sons for inspection, and where there was more than one son who was old enough to be a boy soldier the mothers were forced to choose which son was to go with the rebels. If the mother refused, the rebels shot one of the children dead. It was an impossible situation to be in and it became even clearer to me why families had fled from around the country and into Freetown. What a choice for a mother to have to make, to decide which son will be a boy soldier, or one of your other children will be shot! Again, the questions from the counsellor were answered by the boy in a manner similar to what had happened during the first interview. The boy had a cockiness and devil-may-care attitude, but eventually ended up in tears – just like the first one. Even to my untrained eye it was obvious that he was severely traumatised. I felt that the whole situation was really screwed up and I was totally out of my depth when it came to dealing with the mental anguish that they were suffering. Getting food to and dealing with starving people was a lot easier than dealing with traumatised children.

The next person into the room was a young girl, about fourteen years old. She described how she had been taken from her village to be a 'wife' for the rebels. She had been raped repeatedly but had eventually managed to escape. I listened to her anguished sobs as she told her story and suddenly it all became too much for me. I sat in to witness some of the interviews to have some understanding of the trauma that people had suffered, as I could be working with many more like them. I had been aware of what had been happening in the country as I had been informed during briefings, but to hear the victims tell their personal stories was hard to take. I was not a counsellor; I was in Sierra Leone to oversee emergency construction. For my part, I had heard enough – I was incredibly upset, so I excused myself and left the room.

I walked across the garden and Moses came running up to me and grabbed my hand. Some of the children were running in and out of the sea and so I headed for the beach. However, as soon as I placed my feet on the sand Moses pulled back and whimpered. He was terrified – whatever he had experienced before he ended up in Lakka was having a terrible effect. Later, when we travelled back to our house I felt an air of despondency in the car. As curfew time arrived we sat down for the evening to watch some videos, but it was not a happy setting. We had seen the results of evil and it had been rained down on children – would they ever be normal again? Would I?

PADDY'S BAR

Toireas was an exceptionally good country director. If I needed support or clarification on some issue she was always there to answer my queries. Otherwise she let me get on with the job. What was even more important, given the nature of the place, was that she looked out for our health, both physical and mental. Early in my deployment she told me that it was important to have some relaxation time and to meet other people, as it was not normal to be locked up each night at 6 p.m. We had our meals together every night and then either read or did some work. At the weekend people watched videos, but we were still locked up at night. Staff from other NGOs and the UN went on Saturday afternoons to a makeshift bar called Paddy's, which was not too far from our house. People gathered at the pub from around 1500 hours onwards and then bailed out just before the curfew cut in. The approach to drinking and driving was relaxed, although the designated driver had to go easy on the beer. Paddy's reminded me in a way of the set-up in Loki, but without the madness and hilarity that existed there. Life was much more serious in Sierra Leone.

Mr Ray Would Like a Monkey

The bar was outdoors and partially covered over by a grass roof. It had been a helicopter landing pad at some stage but was now the focal point for people working around Lumley. It was run by an Englishman, but we joked that it was our own Irish pub. Toireas had said that I needed some male company and so she introduced me to people in Paddy's that she was sure I would get on with. My drinking buddies were a Protestant minister from Canada and Father Jude, a Roman Catholic priest from Ireland, and the three of us really hit it off together. Both men had lots of stories to tell, especially Jude, as he had been running the teacher training college for many years.

The clergyman's family had recently been evacuated, but he had opted to stay on with his flock. He told us a story one afternoon about his young son who was aged seven. We had been discussing prejudice and how children got on with other children, irrespective of race, creed or colour. They don't see any difference and he was making the case that you had to learn to be prejudiced. His son had been in school locally, but the family had travelled home to Canada at Christmas. Before they left Freetown, a class photograph was taken and his son showed this photograph to friends and relatives when he got back to Canada. He held up the photograph and declared, 'That's me in the middle of the front row.' He had completely ignored the fact that he was easily identifiable, as he was the only white child in the photograph!

War zones make strange bedfellows and the idea of a Catholic priest and a Protestant clergyman being my drinking buddies all felt very normal and I was very happy with the arrangement. The pub, because of its international clientele, attracted many local prostitutes. Jude commented on them and said, 'Sure God love them, they have to get money somewhere.' They never came near us, as I am sure that they knew who Jude was. They were just allowed to get on with their business.

The time at Paddy's used to fly and in no time at all the dreaded 1800 hours approached, at which time the cars leaving Paddy's bar were like the beginning of the Le Mans twenty-four-hour race. People scrambled from the bar, ran to their cars and took off down the road. There was a security road block a short distance away, but the soldiers were used to the mad evacuation and kept the barriers up and waved all cars though. After my first visit to Paddy's bar we went back to our compound and a feeling of apathy came over me. I had enjoyed my short time out socialising, but now was locked up again for the night. As it was a Saturday night we had some beer and wine in the house and settled down to watch some videos. We had to make the best of our situation, but it was not easy.

A BIT MORE PLANNING, A LOT LESS HASSLE

Back on the work front it soon became clear that, with all the operations going on, a new structure was needed for dealing with the various sites. Logistics could be very easily overwhelmed by the demands for different goods and our transport was limited to just a few pick-ups. James, the logistician, was run ragged, as each site demanded more and more. By speeding up the decision-making we were increasing the demand for more supplies. I called a meeting with the foremen and the engineer and we came to a joint decision about when site meetings would take place. The new arrangement was that at each site meeting we would discuss the planning for the next seven days, prepare the requisitions for all supplies and hand over the paperwork to logistics. One day per week would be designated for each site where that site had priority for supplies and problem-solving. If they had supply problems on any other day, they had to explain at the next site meeting why they had not included the supplies in their weekly plan. This approach focused minds and took the pressure off the logistician, who was responsible for purchasing materials and put the onus for planning on the people running the sites.

Within one week of the new approach, the sites were running much more smoothly. This is the type of approach that is often needed in emergency situations. The local staff are often so traumatised by all that has happened that they have trouble thinking in a logical manner. When someone new comes in, they hopefully have a clear head.

Mr Ray Would Like a Monkey

THE PACE QUICKENS

At a certain point we were asked to speed up the building of the temporary accommodation in Murraytown, as an increasing number of amputees were being discharged from Connaught Hospital in Freetown. They were initially brought to the hospital and treated there, but then moved on to us in Murraytown. We agreed to build faster if we could get more carpenters. The foreman assured me that there was plenty of labour available, as half of the population of the country now seemed to be in Freetown. We decided that an additional 30 carpenters were required. The word was put out and the next morning over 40 new carpenters were at the camp looking for a job. We employed them all by sending the surplus to Approved School, where we had 80 temporary shelters under construction.

However, sometimes when you solve one problem you create another. The delivery of plastic sheeting for the temporary shelters became an issue due to the increased production. The sheeting was given to Concern by the UN, who had it in storage with another NGO. Before it was released to us we had to get approval for our request from the UN and then arrange collection with a pick-up. The sheeting consisted of rolls of heavy-duty plastic that was very bulky, so we could take only two or three rolls in a pick-up at a time. As the time lost in making numerous collections was considerable, it became obvious that we needed to improve our delivery system.

I approached Toireas about streamlining the procedure for getting the sheeting from the UN. I wanted to collect the rolls in bulk and put them into our own store and then issue them to our sites in large quantities, using a truck instead of a pick-up. This would result in less time spent on the road and free up a pick-up. She listened to what I had to say and then asked me to set out the quantity of what we wanted, with backup details. Within a few hours of handing over the details to her she was back from the UN with approval for us to collect all the rolls that we needed for the next month. It was great to have someone who could cut through the red tape and keep matters moving at the accelerated pace.

A SMALL FAVOUR

Murraytown was designated as a camp for amputees and their dependents, but sometimes someone would just arrive and settle down wherever they could find a place to stay. On several occasions I noticed an elderly man and woman sitting beside one of the large communal houses that had been constructed during the first phase of providing shelter. There was a small recess about three metres long by two metres wide on one side of the building that resulted in walls of plastic on three sides. The roof of the building projected over the recessed area and gave some shelter from the rain but provided no privacy for the couple who slept on the ground in the recess.

They never requested any assistance from me, but I was concerned that they were exposed to the elements. One morning I asked the site foreman to put up some plastic sheeting at the front of the alcove to give them some space and privacy. They were not amputees and so did not qualify for a place in the existing big shelters or the smaller units we were building. I travelled on to another site but called back the next morning and saw that nothing had been done to close in the alcove. I became a bit annoyed and asked the foremen why the work had not been carried out. We exchanged some words, but basically he told me that he was busy and up to his eyes with amputees. He asked why I was so concerned about two people who should not have been in the camp anyway. I asked him if he had a mother and father and he told me that as far as he knew, they were still alive. But he had not heard from them, so they could have been killed, what with all the recent attacks. His answer stopped me in my tracks. I told him that I hoped that his family were safe, but if his parents were in some camp, wouldn't he want someone to look out for them and give them shelter? I had thoughts of my own mother, who had recently passed away. Not surprisingly, we were both a bit upset after the conversation and he said that he would arrange the work for the following day.

When I went back to the house that night Toireas asked me what was wrong, as I seemed a bit down. I told her that I had become upset at seeing the old couple and felt a bit emotional about it all.

'I have been surrounded by amputees all day and yet I got upset that an old man and woman are homeless,' I said. 'That's OK 'she said, 'The day that you don't get upset is the day we will get worried about you. It is impossible to be detached all the time.'

The next day the alcove had been enclosed and the old couple were sitting quietly in their new 'home,' with some of the plastic sheeting pulled back to form a makeshift door. I felt happy for them.

LUCY

Lucy (not her real name) was a little girl who was about four years of age and lived at Murraytown Camp with her mother. I noticed her on my first day at the camp. She was a pretty little thing with big dark eyes that looked very sad. She clung with her left hand to a stuffed Cookie Monster toy from the *Sesame Street* show. Most of her right arm was missing and she had shrapnel scars along her ribs. Whenever I saw Lucy I would say hello and smile, but she never smiled back or answered. She just clung to Cookie Monster as if her life depended on it.

One day her mother, who would have been in her mid-twenties and looked tired and worn out, came over to me and started to tell me their story. The family had been in their village when it was attacked by the RUF with AK-47 assault rifles. People scattered and ran in every direction. Lucy's grandmother picked her up and ran with her in her arms, but the grandmother was killed, and Lucy wounded. She was then grabbed by her mother, who bent over and ran as fast as she could. 'They shot me as well, but I kept running,' her mother said. She turned around and pulled her shirt up to show me her back, which had three welts where bullets had scorched her skin. If she had not been bent over the three bullets would have torn right through her and killed her. A bullet had struck Lucy in her mid-upper arm and such was the force of the high velocity bullet that it blew most of her arm off. Mother and child eventually ended up in Connaught Hospital and were then moved on to us in Murraytown Camp. She did not know if her husband was alive or dead but thought that he had probably been killed in the attack. After that initial meeting we would wave or say hello whenever we met.

One evening, as we had our dinner back in the house, I was told that there was some bad news from Murraytown. The mother had died suddenly that afternoon. I really felt the loss. Lucy had no other relatives in the camp, so she was now a four-year-old UAC (unaccompanied child). One of the other families in the camp took over minding her, but I wondered at the time just how much unhappiness one child could bear. She was just one among many and yet I can still see her clearly, hugging the Cookie Monster with her one good arm. Some memories are impossible to erase.

WATERLOO

Waterloo was located near the frontline and there was an old airstrip from the Second World War close by. In the wet season there is considerable rainfall in Sierra Leone and the clay surface quickly turns into a muddy mess. Setting up camp around a concrete airstrip made life easier for the displaced and so a large camp had grown up there very quickly. Unfortunately, the rebels had recently attacked it and sprayed the place with automatic gunfire.

The 'houses' consisted of mud-built walls with bush sticks and plastic sheets for roofs and we received a report that lots of the houses had been damaged in the latest attack. The main problem was that the bullets had ripped holes through the mud walls and plastic sheeting and so were no longer watertight. The locals had repaired the walls in most cases, but we had been asked to assess the damage and put forward a plan for the roof repairs.

Mr Ray Would Like a Monkey

The journey to Waterloo took several hours – it was just over twenty miles from our office, but the roads were jammed with traffic as there were military road blocks every half mile. I decided to count the roadblocks on my first trip and found that there were over 40. When we eventually arrived at the camp I found that it was in a lovely setting. There were thousands of palm trees and there were houses built amongst the trees as far as the eye could see. Within minutes of leaving our car and walking among the houses I was disoriented and hadn't a clue where I was. There were trees everywhere and I quickly lost my sense of direction. How on earth are we going to do an assessment here, was my first thought. Our car was parked on the airstrip and the driver's job was to monitor the radio in case of a security alert and to get us away as quickly as possible if the need arose, but where the car and driver were was a mystery to me. The engineer could obviously see that I was unsettled and said that we should not go too far into the camp. After we had examined several houses it quickly became clear that what we needed was a total figure for the number of damaged roofs. Once we had that information we would know how much plastic sheeting was required. I asked the engineer about collecting the required information because as far as I could see there was no logical pattern to the layout of the houses. He calmly indicated that he knew that there were around two thousand houses in total and so we just needed to get several assessment teams together to establish the number that were damaged. I could see the assessment taking weeks, but he said that he would have the report ready in a few days and meanwhile we should start planning transport and storage for the job. There was a forty-foot container nearby that no one seemed to own and so we claimed it for our site office and store. I arranged for several chairs and a table to be sent to the site and heavy locks for the large steel doors.

After a few days the engineer told me that the number of damaged roofs had been confirmed from each team and I headed out to the site to check the details. We sat in the 'office' and it was like an oven. The doors were wide open and the desk and chairs were just a few feet inside the container. I had seen containers used in Kenya as offices and stores but the secret to making them habitable was to construct an apex roof over the container. The roofs there had been made of timber and straw with a large overhang on all sides that provided shade and windows cut into the sides of the containers to create air flow. We had not got around to these refinements here and so were working in an overheated steel box.

I sat down to examine the reports on the damage and was pleasantly surprised to see that the reports were classified under separate headings of A, B, C, D etc. Under each letter there were dozens and dozens of houses listed. I was really impressed and asked how they managed to identify all the houses so quickly. The engineer said that it was quite easy, but I was still not convinced and so I picked a few random samples from the list and asked him to show me the damaged roofs. He quickly led me to the houses and when I asked how he knew which house was which, he just smiled and pointed to a letter and number carved into the mud wall, high above the doorway.

'The site was divided into sections, just like we are doing at Approved School, and each section has a designating letter, A, B, C etc.,' he said. 'The houses were numbered as they were built, so in A section we have A1, A2, A3 etc. Otherwise we wouldn't be able to tell one house from another.'

I felt like a bit of a fool – how had I missed the obvious? These guys were switched on and I could learn a lot if I paid a bit more attention. When we totalled the various sections, there were over 900 roofs that had been damaged in the attack. With an average of five people per house that meant that almost 5000 people, mostly women and children, were living in accommodation with rain pouring in on top of them. Now that we had the figures, we could start to put together a plan to remedy that problem.

THE BEACH HOUSE

At home in Ireland I had walked a lot and enjoyed the feeling that comes from regular exercise. The chances of getting much exercise in Freetown were reduced, because of the 6 p.m. curfew, so I tried to make the most of what limited time there was and decided that instead of driving home from the office each night, I would walk whenever possible. Beth and Toireas could each drive home, so we had transport at the house. If there was going to be an evacuation, transport was not needed, as the helipad was within walking distance. A car would be no use in that situation anyway.

I enjoyed the walk in the evening, although the temperature and humidity meant that I was covered in sweat within minutes of setting out. I found that the people who lived on my route home were very friendly and many greeted me with a smile. Although many spoke English, the local language, Krio, a form of pidgin English, is quite easy to understand. I would occasionally hear a shout of, 'Hey man, how de bodi?' which is really self-explanatory. My reply of, 'de bodi gud,' also spoke volumes, although some days my body wasn't actually feeling too good. I met Father Jude in Paddy's bar one Saturday and told him that I was walking home from work whenever possible, but would like to get a bit more exercise. He suggested that I go swimming at the weekend, but I told him that the last time I had tried that I had nearly been shot. He told me about an area of beach out near the teacher training college where he worked and that as the spot was out of sight of the main beach it should be safe. He had the keys for a beach house and suggested that we go out the following Sunday and see the place, which we duly did. The beach house consisted of one small room and a toilet, so it suited us perfectly.

Toireas and Catherine weren't too pushed about the swimming, but Beth and I took to the sea and enjoyed the experience. Jude agreed to leave the keys of the beach house with a local man when we needed them, so all we had to do was phone Jude beforehand. The owners were from France and were unlikely to visit in the near future. I was delighted with the arrangement and swimming at the weekend became a regular pastime. Toireas was good at getting people together and she came up with the idea of having a picnic there one Sunday. We invited people from a few other NGOs and the UN and a 'gentleman, David,' from the British High Commission. We had a lovely time and I enjoyed chatting with 'David', who asked a lot of questions about the work that we were involved in. He expressed an interest in seeing the camp set-up at Murraytown and I invited him to visit during the week, which he did. Little did I realise at the time that he would be a key person in facilitating the construction of the rehabilitation unit that was badly needed for the amputees.

FUNDING

We needed money to carry out the various jobs involved, whether it was construction of emergency shelter or the health programme, and funding for the various projects was tightly controlled. The people providing the money are referred to as donors. The basic process is that a budget is set for all the operations and we have to adhere to it. The accountant was the bane of my life because when I saw something that needed to be done, my instinct was to go ahead and do it. The unfortunate accountant, however, had to make sure that the money required was allocated in the budget and keep a tight rein on me – not an easy task when I was fired up.

Funding for the work can come from many sources, but the basic procedure is that a proposal is prepared and supporting documentation, including costings, are submitted to Head Office, who then allocate funds if they're available. Head Office obtained funds from voluntary donations and sent requests to various groups and countries to finance the work. The Irish Department of Foreign Affairs has a specialist unit that deals with such requests, as have many other countries. The European Community also provide funding and in some cases the UN provide food or non-food items that are distributed by NGOs. On occasions a donor may agree to fund a percentage of the work, which means that the balance of the money required has to be found elsewhere. In this way there may be several donors involved in any one project and this means several reports have to be prepared each month. Having several donors can make life a bit more difficult, especially if the monthly reports to the donors have different cut-off dates. It is a complex business putting a package together and not something that I wanted to be involved in too deeply, but I did have to be aware of the various constraints.

The complexity surrounding the allocation of funds for specific projects was brought home to me when Handicap International (HI), who made prosthetic limbs, asked for a rehabilitation unit to be built in Murraytown. I sat down with the Swiss guy in charge and we agreed measurements for what was required. We then tried to find a suitable location on the site, but all the level ground was already taken up. It seemed that we would have to construct the unit on a sloping site that had various drainage culverts. I consulted with our engineer and a suitable layout was prepared and agreed with Handicap International. It seemed that it was full speed ahead.

However, before we could start we needed permission from the Finance Section and I was informed that there was no money allocated for a rehab unit. I discussed the matter with the accountant, but she told me that the money allocated for construction was for shelter, latrines and kitchens, so we would have to apply for separate funding. I was a bit annoyed because the amputees needed the facility as soon as possible, but of course the accountant was correct, we could only spend what had been approved.

Toireas very quickly stepped in and prepared a proposal to forward to the Dublin office. Within a few days I had a nice surprise. She had met the gentleman from the British High Commission who had been at our picnic and he had asked how I was and how the work was progressing in the various camps. She told him about the proposed rehab unit and that I was frustrated at not being able to start work straight away while we waited for funding approval. 'Tell him to start building, the British government had funds available for such work and I will organise that,' was the reply.

A pleasant chat at a picnic had resulted in the amputees getting what they needed. I really appreciated the support.

www.southdublinlibraries.ie

South Dublin Libraries

North West 200

When I was at home, one of my pastimes was motorcycling and I loved being involved in the Irish road racing scene. The week of the North West 200 motorcycle races in Portstewart, Portrush and Coleraine was an event that I loved to attend and was one of the highlights of my year. When I had agreed to go to Sierra Leone I felt that I would miss being at the event and was looking forward to getting emails from home telling me all that was happening. As it turned out, I was so busy on the Saturday of the races that I hardly had time to think about what was going on at home.

Before I had arrived a lot of temporary shelters had already been constructed by various NGOs. There was a problem with some of the roofs when the high winds, associated with tropical storms, blew ferociously. Plastic sheeting was ripped from the roofs on some units. The problem was identified and remedial work started, but this had to be done in conjunction with the building of new units. The day before the North West 200 I was informed that a storm had damaged the roofs on some existing units and was asked to arrange for the repairs to be carried out over the weekend. One of the roofs being repaired had housed a woman and a baby and she came out from her neighbour's unit to talk to me. She told me that she had given birth to a little girl during the storm and hoped that the roof would be repaired quickly. I asked her the baby's name and she told me that she had not named her yet, so I asked if I could suggest a name. She gave me a big smile and asked me what name I had in mind.

'Elizabeth,' I said, 'my wife's name'.

'Dat be gud,' she said, and I felt a lump in my throat.

I was sitting on an overturned barrel in the middle of a camp and was suddenly missing my family. Homesickness can strike that way – a sudden feeling of the blues and there is nothing you can do about it. The North West 200 did not seem that important anymore.

Mr Ray Would Like a Monkey

Connaught Hospital

The main hospital in Freetown was a large colonial-style building near the city centre and Beth had been invited by a German nurse, Sonya from MSF, to visit the hospital and see the situation there first-hand. Beth asked me if I would like to accompany her, as a lot of the patients who were there would eventually end up in Murraytown. When we arrived at the hospital I saw an In/Out board just inside the entrance. In/Out indicated whether the doctors, all local, were present or not. All the Out boxes were ticked. It was not a good situation, I felt. Sonya explained that since the attack on Freetown by the RUF, the hospital depended almost entirely on MSF doctors.

First, we were shown around some of the operating theatres. They were very basic and did not have the high-tech finishes or equipment that Westerners take for granted. Cleaning staff were hosing blood off the concrete floors. The next stop on the tour was the adult male ward. Some of the patients waved at us and said hello. A doctor approached a man who was lying on a bed with both of his legs heavily bandaged. There was a very strong smell coming from the legs and the patient looked up at the doctor and asked what was going to happen to him.

'You were lying out in the bush for too long with gunshot wounds. You have gangrene in both legs so we will have to amputate them,' replied the doctor.

'When?' asked the patient.

'Soon,' replied the doctor, 'probably tomorrow.'

The patient lifted his arm and shook hands with the doctor and thanked him. I was quite shocked at the acceptance that the patient had shown. There were several more patients awaiting amputations, as well as patients who had been chopped and needed their wounds tidied up. To this day the smell of gangrene is something that I cannot forget.

Beth and Sonya chatted away and then the nurse suggested that we go up to the first floor. Sonya looked at me and then said to Beth, 'I think that he is a first-floor sort of guy and will be alright.' I wasn't following the conversation at all and asked what was on the first floor.

'Children's' ward,' she replied.

I thought that I was prepared for nearly anything at this stage, but the large number of children in the ward was a huge shock. Most of the small children were two or three to a bed and were suffering from various ailments. Some had been shot or been wounded with shrapnel. One girl was sitting with her mother on a bed and staring into space. One side of her face was very badly swollen and she had a dressing around her head. Sonya explained that the child's ear had been chopped off with a machete and the wound had become infected. It had taken several days to get to the hospital, as they tried to avoid the RUF when they were travelling. The child would not speak. She reminded me of Moses out in Lakka – totally traumatised. As I drove back to the house all I could see was the frightened face of a nine-year-old girl – what threat had she been to anyone? I felt helpless in the face of such atrocities.

A SPECIAL MEETING

Monday morning was the designated day for Murraytown site meetings. It was the closest camp to the office and so the week kicked off there. I had just arrived and was having a look around with the foreman when one of the elderly men in the camp asked to see me. The camp had elected a camp committee and it was through this committee that requests from the residents were processed. This man was their spokesperson. Sometimes it was just something simple that was required, like having an extra latrine dug, and we could get on with that straight away. If it was something bigger, then we had to look at budgets and see what could be done. My heart sank when the elder came up to me and asked if I would attend a meeting. I was imagining another list of requests that were going to be added to our workload and it was only the start of the week.

As I walked across the camp and saw a gathering of quite a few people I thought that whatever was up had to be quite serious.

Mr Ray Would Like a Monkey

I asked the foreman if there was anything major and he seemed as puzzled as I was. The spokesperson called for quiet and started to make a speech. He spoke of the terrible situation in their country and of the terrible things that had happened. At this stage I was apprehensive and expected to hear a major complaint about something or other. The worst part was not knowing what was coming next. I was pleasantly surprised though when he smiled and said that matters had improved greatly since Concern had arrived and that the camp inhabitants wanted to thank us for all our work. I was a bit taken aback, as this was the last thing I had expected.

I was asked to step forward and the elder announced, 'I would like to thank Mr Ray for helping us and ask him to accept a gift from the camp.'

A young boy stepped forward from the crowd and with a smile handed me a bottle of Coke.

I was much moved and with a lump in my throat thanked them. I was stunned. What had happened was the last thing I would have expected. They had practically nothing, had suffered terrible trauma, and yet had thought of me.

It was the strangest ceremony that I had ever witnessed – I drank some of the Coke, after which there was a round of cheering and those who had two hands clapped them together, and those with just one hand clapped on their arms. I was humbled, I was with friends. The bottle was returned and the bottle cap safely stored to be used as a makeshift washer in the construction of the roofs on the temporary dwellings. Nothing was wasted in Freetown.

LAUGHTER, THE BEST MEDICINE

After the initial shock of being surrounded by amputees in Murray-town, I settled down and was very much at home in the camp. For some strange reason, the occupants appeared to be reasonably happy, despite their situation, and this rubbed off on me. There was still lots of work to be done, but hearing people laughing helped to lift my spirits and at times they certainly needed lifting.

Work on the new rehabilitation unit was progressing after the surprise funding, but until that building was completed the old building on-site continued to be used for various purposes. I called in to the old building one morning to see the technician. There was a small waiting area and I sat down on one of the chairs, glad to be out of the sun and to get a break for a few minutes. There were several amputees sitting around waiting to see the technician and to be measured for their prosthetic limbs. There were some able-bodied children playing around the camp and wandering in and out of the waiting room and they seemed fascinated by the prosthetics lying on a table. The arms were sample prosthetics consisting of a partial forearm and hand and were left- and right-handed.

While I was waiting a man came into the unit, looked around and chatted with some of the occupants. Both his arms had been amputated about six inches above his wrists. He carefully studied the various prosthetic limbs on the table. He then slid his stumps into the prosthetics, not without difficulty, but put the left stump into the right prosthetic and the right stump into the left. He chuckled to himself and suddenly turned around and waved the wrong-handed limbs at the children and shouted, 'Aaahh!'

The children screamed and took flight and the man roared laughing. I got a bit of a shock initially, but then started to laugh, as did everyone else in the room. Someone said that the children would be having terrible nightmares that night and we laughed even more. The technician came out and asked what was going on and we had trouble telling him as we were all laughing so much. Suddenly life did not seem so bad after all. Laughter was indeed the best medicine! I hope that those children are not still having nightmares.

THE ROADBLOCK

A short time later I was reminded of getting left and right mixed up. As part of our daily security precautions we checked with the UN for security updates. The riskiest trip was travelling to Waterloo, as it was a long way from the office and close to the front line.

During our time at that site the driver always stayed with the car and listened carefully for any security warnings coming in over the short-wave radio. One morning I was informed in the office that there had been an attack on a checkpoint near Waterloo and to approach the area with caution. The roadblock in that location usually closed off the entire road and verge on the right-hand side. This meant that we had to go off the road on the left-hand side, drive along the grass verge and then return to the road beyond the obstruction. We were required to approach the checkpoint slowly and only proceed when directed. The troops seemed a bit tense and the driver was noticeably nervous too when we stopped. After a few questions we were told to proceed and to go to the right of the roadblock. The driver took off, but instead of going to the right he drove across the road towards the left-hand side, our usual route. The troops started to shout and guns were raised and pointed in our direction. I immediately pulled on the handbrake and at the same time shouted at the driver to stop.

The driver's door was whipped open and a gun shoved in at him as they screamed, 'We told you to go right.'

The driver was quaking as he pointed with his left hand and replied, 'I did go right.'

It suddenly dawned on me that he couldn't distinguish between left and right. I tried to calm the situation down, apologised and explained that the driver was very nervous because of the earlier attack and he mixed up his right and left. They were not happy, they were jumpy, but after a few minutes they let us travel on. By the time we reached the camp at Waterloo I was still quite shaken and had difficulty concentrating on the job in hand. The return trip was uneventful, but when I got back to the house that night I had trouble wiping out the memory and realised that both of us could have been shot. Just something else to look out for to stay safe.

ON STANDBY

The security situation remained serious throughout the country. We would often hear about the latest atrocities and the general population was nervous, to say the least. Would the RUF attack Freetown again and, if so, what would be the outcome? For the international aid workers, evacuation at short notice was a real possibility.

Our house in Aberdeen was one of the designated meet-up points for evacuation if the need arose. The code name for our house was McDonald's. Another evacuation point was code-named Burger King. I have often wondered who it was that dreamed up the code names and had concluded that the person on this occasion was an American – or was I being unfair? The most dangerous place for us to travel to, without doubt, had to be Waterloo, as it was so close to the front line and just over twenty miles from the office. Twenty miles might not seem much but when the roads were jammed with traffic it could take several hours to cover that distance. Along the side of the main roads were mile markers – large stones with a number carved into them. This number indicated the distance in miles from Freetown. The British had arranged for a ship from the Royal Navy to be stationed off Freetown and we could clearly see it from our house.

On board the ship were helicopters designated to collect us at McDonald's, Burger King and other evacuation points if the rebels got to the 16-mile marker. I had observed the ship as it sailed back and forth parallel to the shore and was reassured that help was nearby if and when we needed it. All our names had been registered with the British High Commission, so nothing would be left to chance when it came to evacuation. The danger with being on constant alert of course is, that you can become somewhat laidback about the risks, so we had to concentrate on being alert to the dangers and at the same time get on with our work. It was a bit of a balancing act, but I was not unduly worried.

On several occasions we had seen a lot of activity on board the ship. When this happened we wondered if something was

Mr Ray Would Like a Monkey

up that we had yet to hear about. The people who carry out these military missions do lots of training so it could have been a training exercise or the real thing. Either way I felt a deep sense of gratitude for the support. Pilots who fly into dangerous situations to rescue people are definitely heroes in my mind.

There had been several false alarms, but late one afternoon we were told that the security situation had deteriorated and that we were to go on standby. We had a visitor staying in our house that night, an English guy who was a new arrival to Sierra Leone. We were sitting in our house, having had dinner, waiting for an update and feeling fairly relaxed. The visitor, however, was very jumpy and kept standing up, walking around and talking incessantly. We tried to calm him down, but the more relaxed we were the more excited he seemed to become. Eventually I told him that whatever happened would be good news from our point of view and he needed to relax.

'How can any of this be good?' he asked.

I informed him that either the rebels would be turned back and that would be good news or they would get past the 16-mile marker and we would be airlifted out. If that happened we would be on a ship instead of being locked down for the night and they would probably feed us and give us a few drinks and we would have someone new to talk to, which would be very nice. Even better, the navy would transport us to Guinea, where there was no curfew and we could go out for the night, which would be a nice experience for a change. I told him to look on the bright side. He didn't say much after that and seemed to calm down – every cloud has a silver lining.

Eventually we got the call to say that the danger was over and to stand down. There would be no evacuation, so we were locked down for the night – again! I figured I would have to go Conakry some other time but as it turned out that would be sooner than I thought.

The Lariam experiment

As mentioned earlier, Sierra Leone was also called 'white man's grave', and not without reason. The chances of becoming ill with some tropical disease were high. Malaria was widespread and typhoid was also high on the list of diseases contracted. Malaria can be a killer disease if not treated in time and so diagnosis and treatment are not something you delay. I had seen first-hand in Sudan how a boy who had been playing football at midday had died by midnight due to malaria. The disease is spread by malaria-carrying mosquitoes biting the skin. They bite where there is a good blood supply, usually the backs of the hands or around the neck. Only the females carry the deadly disease and they attack at night-time, so for protection we used mosquito nets over our beds and fine mesh over the windows, as well as repellent on our skin. There were no injections to give protection and taking prophylaxis tablets minimised the risk but did not guarantee that you would not get the disease.

On my posting to Kenya and Sudan I had been prescribed two different types of tablets, chloroquine and paludrine. Chloroquine was taken once a week, while paludrine was taken daily. The daily tablet could cause stomach upsets and so it was not unusual to have bouts of diarrhoea. The weekly tablet resulted in nice dreams, but only on the night that I took it. I was certainly experiencing a lot of problems with stomach complaints and I put this down to the tablets. Some people were prescribed tablets based on mefloquine, which is marketed under the trade name Lariam. A doctor in Dublin had suggested I use it when in Sierra Leone as it offered better resistance than the combined doses of paludrine and chloroquine against the strain of malaria found in West Africa. I had heard lots of stories about Lariam and the strange ways different people reacted to the drug. Some seemed to be unaffected while others became quite aggressive and argumentative, so I turned down the suggestion and stuck with what I knew.

However, after a while in Freetown and due to continuing stomach problems, I decided that maybe Lariam might be a better bet and decided to give it a try. I took my first Lariam tablet on a Sunday night and that was my first week covered. I had discussed the change in medication with Beth as she was the health specialist and she informed me that she was on Lariam too, and I could see that it was not affecting her negatively. She was in no way aggressive and was in fact one of the calmest people around, so I was hopeful. I asked her to keep an eye on me and to let me know if she thought that I was behaving oddly, to which she replied, 'How will we know?' and laughed.

I spent the rest of the week working away and the diarrhoea eased off, but I did experience the vivid dreams that other people had spoken of. I felt at times that I was being dragged out of bed and would wake up shouting at the non-existent person who was doing the dragging. Some of the dreams were terrifying and by the end of the week I was worn out from all the nightmares. Clearly Lariam did not work for me and so after that first week I decided to go back on my usual tablets and took the chloro-quine and paludrine on the Sunday night.

Later I was reading a book when I suddenly felt tired and a bit out of sorts. I stood up, said goodnight and threw the book across the floor rather than placing it on the table. Why did I do that? I thought.

Nobody said anything, but I could see some puzzled looks. I went up the stairs to my room and got into bed. I felt terribly tired, almost exhausted. I started to drift off to sleep, but just as I was on the verge of nodding off my body would tremble all over for a few seconds and I would be wide awake again. This happened several times and I became extremely nervous. I spent about two hours in bed unable to go asleep. I had started to fall asleep on several occasions, but as I was on the point of dropping off I would be woken by the twitching and trembling.

I was exhausted, but the situation got worse. I started having weird thoughts and decided that I would go for a walk on the beach. I knew that would be crazy due to the curfew, but then thought, OK, I will get a knife and then go for a walk. It was like there were two people in my body, one was instructing me to go and do something really stupid and another person who was saying no, no, no! I thought that I was having a nervous breakdown and was surprised that it had happened so suddenly. I got up out of bed and went downstairs but everyone seemed to have retired for the night. I knocked on Beth's door and when she came out I told her that I was unwell and thought that I was going out of my mind.

She sat down and asked me calmly to describe what was happening. Toireas and Catherine appeared and listened to me and I could see that they were worried. Beth told them it was alright and that she would stay with me. She told them to go back to bed and that she would call them if she needed help. She explained to me that she thought my condition had something to do with the Lariam.

That made me feel a little bit better, but I was still having thoughts of going out into the night with a knife. I was no longer tired and was actually afraid of myself.

'Keep telling me what you're thinking and feeling,' she said, and so began a long night of talking and her persuading me to stay in the house. Several times she asked me if I was tired and if I would consider going back to bed, but I was terrified at the thought. As long as I was awake and kept indoors I would be safe, and with her help I could keep the 'other me' under control. We sat up until 6 a.m., at which stage the poor woman was exhausted and I agreed that I would go back to bed. The curfew ended in an hours' time, so I would be safe after that. I went back to bed, fell asleep and woke an hour later, full of beans and ready for work. Beth was on the phone when I came down for my breakfast and I heard her explaining to someone what had happened. After a few minutes she turned and asked me how I was.

'Great,' I said, 'OK now and ready for work, thanks.'

She explained that she had been talking to a doctor in MSF and had given him the whole story and that he had diagnosed the problem. After taking the Lariam for a week there was still

Mr Ray Would Like a Monkey

some in my system and I should have waited before going back on the chloroquine and paludrine. I had overdosed by taking the different drugs too close together and this had sent me out of my mind. After breakfast Toireas put me in the car and drove me to a different doctor. I told him my story and he agreed with the diagnosis that had been given over the phone. He said that it must have been very frightening. I agreed.

'How do you feel now?' he asked.

'Great, great,' I said, 'can't wait to get to work.'

'You're high,' he said. 'We will have to slow you down,' and he produced some Valium and made me take it there and then. He maintained that it would take a few days for the mixture of drugs to work their way out of my system. There was a danger that I could go a bit weird when I tried to go to sleep and so he prescribed a large dose of Mogadon sleeping tablets. He informed Toireas of the amount he was prescribing and said to make sure that I was in bed when I took them.

We headed back to the office and I was grounded for the day. I had lots to do and had to write up the minutes of several site meetings, as well as other work. I was not a fast typist, but that day I had the minutes written up in no time and was surprised to find that I hardly needed to refer to my notes as the discussions that had taken place on-site were easily recalled. I was a bit frightened by it all and worried that I would have a repeat episode that night.

We headed back to the house at the end of the day and after dinner it was suggested that I should go to bed early as I had had only one hour's sleep the night before. Beth and Toireas told me to get into bed and that they would bring up my sleeping tablets.

'That will put you to sleep alright, no sitting up tonight.' they laughed.

I took the Mogadon, was asleep within seconds and slept soundly all night. I had to continue on the prescribed medication for the rest of the week, by which time I had slowed down and could go to bed without being afraid that I would try and go out in the curfew. I was very aware that my life had probably been saved by the patience and bravery of a Canadian nurse. However, when I said this to her a few days later she just smiled and said that it wasn't that bad, as if sitting up with a guy who was off his head and who was looking for a sharp knife was just part of the job. Heroes come in all shapes and sizes.

BETH'S CLINIC

Beth was based in Approved School camp where we were providing shelter for about four thousand people. The building programme there was proceeding well and people were being housed as the units were completed. The arrangement was that we would construct the units and provide the auxiliary services, including kitchens and latrines. Oxfam had constructed a water supply system and the speed with which they had worked was incredibly impressive. Without doubt, they were the experts when it came to a good water supply. Once the water was established we built concrete bases to facilitate washing or laundry slabs, as they were called. A community was being established.

We did not have a say as to which families were to be housed in the units, as this was supposed to be arranged by a government 'housing department.' However, in practice the camp inhabitants themselves agreed on who went into the units. A camp committee had been formed and matters were discussed and worked out by them as far as possible. Preference was given to families with babies and small children. However, once the preferred method of allocation became common knowledge we had the strange situation of people placing babies in the partially constructed units to stake their claim on a unit. We had to step in and stop this very quickly, due to the obvious danger, and advised that the units could not be occupied until the roofs went on.

The health needs of all these displaced people were handled by Beth and a small team of local helpers. Beth had asked me to look at the clinic on-site, which was just a small room and looked as if it had been previously used for storing equipment at the school. It was obviously far too small but was all that was immediately available. There had been a bigger building, but it had been blown up and all that remained of it was a concrete base. If we could put up another building on the concrete base, it would certainly improve the situation. I measured up the concrete base and prepared a drawing and we then sat down and designed a new clinic that would cater better for the needs on-site. Some people have problems in reading a drawing and visualising what a building will look like on the ground, but this was not the case with Beth. She knew what was required and a plan was drawn that met with her approval. The building was to be constructed in brick and to have a roof of cast-iron sheeting. The internal layout was to be sub-divided in such a way that the partitions could be easily removed at some time in the future if the building was required for a different purpose. This required careful considera-tion in relation to where the windows were to be placed, but very quickly the design was agreed, materials ordered, and construc-tion commenced.

'Beth's Clinic' was what was written on the drawings, and that was what the building became known as – it was a fitting tribute to all her hard work.

A SUDDEN STOP

Work was going well on all fronts and I was happy. I was back on the paludrine and chloroquine and had to put up with the side effects, but at least I was able to sleep at night. The shelter programme at Murraytown was nearly finished and the reha-bilitation unit there was under construction. Approved School was progressing well and lots of families were now under cover. I was even able to go for an occasional swim at the weekend and was getting some exercise. What could go wrong?

One Saturday morning I felt like I was getting the flu. My throat was a bit sore and I had a headache. I returned to the house at lunchtime and decided to go to bed and sleep it off. I woke up around teatime and felt worse. I had a pounding headache, ached all over and was sweating more than usual. I had a shower and then went down to the kitchen to get a drink. Beth was there preparing some dinner. She commented that I looked unwell and told me to take things easy. I had some food and read for a while, but a few hours later I felt a lot worse.

'I'm going to take a blood sample from you and get it tested in the morning,' said Beth. 'I think you have malaria.'

The blood sample was taken and a film of blood smeared onto two glass slides and put to one side. We would have to wait until the curfew was lifted in the morning, after which the slides would be delivered to the doctor for testing. I decided to return to bed as I felt that I was becoming sicker by the minute, but at least I had two good nurses to look after me.

Beth and Toireas checked on me regularly and my temperature went up and up. I was covered in sweat and felt like I was on fire. They told me to get out of bed and have a cold shower to cool down, which I did. They made regular checks on me and filled in a score card that was used to help with the diagnosis of malaria. The raging heat started to lessen but then I started to feel really cold and ended up shivering, a condition called rigor. They got all the spare blankets in the house and put them on my bed, but I was still shivering. A short time later my temperature started to rise and in no time I was soaking and needed to be cooled down again. After a while, the information from the score cards indicated that malaria was a strong possibility and a decision was made to treat me. The blood test would confirm if the diagnosis was correct or not but waiting for treatment was not an option at that stage. We had some Fansidar tablets in our emergency kit and they gave them to me – this was one of the recommended treatments for malaria.

The cycle of fever and rigor continued and as the night wore on I was convinced that I was going to die. I got quite angry and I suppose a bit irrational. I don't want to die in this place, was all I thought. I want to die in my own bed at home. The fact that it would be better to be alive at home was not an option I considered at that stage, as I was convinced that it would all be over soon. I dozed on and off and when the curfew ended Beth told me that she was on her way to the doctor with my blood sample. I got out of bed, expecting someone to take me to hospital,

Mr Ray Would Like a Monkey

but within a short time Beth arrived back, accompanied by the doctor. It was the same man I had seen after my Lariam experience. He greeted me with a smile and told me that the bad news was that I had falciparum malaria, which was very serious, but the good news was that the Fansidar would sort it out and I would be fine eventually. I felt that my life had been saved yet again and knew that if I had been on my own, the outcome could have been very different.

I expected some long drawn-out procedure, as I felt terrible, but all I needed now was to drink lots of fluids and get plenty of rest.

'No alcohol,' he warned.

My treatment was complete! Hundreds of thousands of people died in Africa every year from malaria and the treatment was that simple. I thought that I would recover quickly. I had only a short time left on my contract and was still hopeful that I could complete most of my work. But over the next few days, as I spent a lot of time sleeping, it soon became clear that I was not going to be fit for work for some time. I went to my favourite place, Murraytown, to see how the rehabilitation unit was progressing, but after only an hour there I was exhausted and had to go back to the house. Some of the staff came to see me, but again I was exhausted after a very short time talking to them. The writing was on the wall and yet I did not want to see the obvious.

I was aware that Beth's contract was almost complete and that she was travelling to Dublin before returning home to Canada. However, when Toireas told me that she wanted me to travel with Beth to Dublin, as I was too ill to continue, I was devastated and felt tears come into my eyes. Malaria can cause people to become quite depressed and I was certainly not a laugh a minute at that stage. I knew that what was being proposed made sense and yet felt terrible about letting people down. I asked if I could stay until the rehab unit was completed but was told that I was the one who now needed help. I would not be fit to travel home on my own, so going with Beth was the obvious answer.

It was such an abrupt change that I had trouble getting my head around it. In just a few days I had gone from being a person happy with all that was going on to a shuffling, weak man who needed help to get back home. I had been thrilled and buzzing when I had first arrived by helicopter in Freetown and now I had to be helped in and out of the aircraft. I was a wreck and all the time I longed for the people who had become my friends, the amputees in Murraytown. It seemed that I needed them as much as they needed me. How had that happened? My memory of the trip back is vague, as I spent most of the time sleeping. Without Beth I would surely have been found asleep in some airport, not too sure where I was.

DUBLIN

Liz met us at Dublin airport and told me afterwards that she was shocked at my appearance and had not recognised me initially. Beth handed me over to Liz and I was driven to a check-up with the tropical medical specialists. Blood samples were taken and various checks made, but I wasn't too sure what was going on. One thing I did know was that I had been in fine trim and full of energy when I had returned from Africa at Christmas, but now six months later I was a shadow of my former self. I told the doctor that I felt that I had let people down, especially as I had not completed the rehab unit. He told me the malaria made me feel that way, that I had to concentrate on getting better and this would take some time. He advised that I should stay away from Africa for at least six months as it could take that long before I was fit again for the hard work involved.

I set about exercising, but it was very frustrating. I had run marathons when I was younger and so walking for long distances had never been a problem, but now I could barely manage half a mile without getting tired and needing to rest. I met a friend one day who said that he had not recognised me at first and wanted to know if I had been sick. I told him what had happened and he said that he was glad to hear that I only had malaria, as looking at me he thought that I had AIDS. I was grateful for small mercies.

Mr Ray Would Like a Monkey

Concern had insisted that I attend a counsellor before and after the posting and so now I had to address that. I was asked about the posting but found that I did not have much to say. I was not aware of this initially, but after a few sessions the counsellor pointed out to me that I deflected when I answered his questions about Sierra Leone and recalled stories about Kenya and Sudan instead. I was home a short time when my father asked me quite innocently what it had been like in Sierra Leone and I surprised myself by saying that I did not want to talk about it. It would be some time before I felt able to tell the story of what it had been like there. My thoughts were that if you hadn't been there you couldn't understand. When it was pointed out to me that I wasn't the first person to feel that way, I felt a bit better, but some experiences can be awfully hard to share initially with people who haven't been in similar situations. After a time, it gets easier.

RETURN TO FREETOWN

It was to be ten years before I returned to Sierra Leone, in 2009, after many more postings in the intervening time. On my first day back in Freetown I asked to be driven to Murraytown. The war was long over and the camp was gone, thank God, but I thought of little Lucy and wondered where she was. We now had lots of development work going on, including building schools, medical centres and running a health programme and lots more besides.

Working on a development programme was very different to working in an emergency setting, but there was still a tremendous need and I found the work hugely satisfying. Beth's Clinic was still in existence and being used as a birthing centre. I called in one day to have a look at the clinic and told the nurse about it being built during the war. After ten years in the tropical weather it looked a bit dilapidated but was still functioning. The building in Lakka that had been used for rehabilitating the child victims of the war was now an orphanage run by an Italian lady who had come to help years before and couldn't leave. I understood that. I spent most of my free time on the beach in Lakka. Waterloo was now a thriving marketplace and I could travel past it without fear of being close to the frontline – there was no frontline. I had reason to visit Connaught Hospital and as I walked through the front doors I clearly recalled the smell of gangrene and the frightened face of a young girl whose ear had been chopped off with a machete. Now there was no curfew, no roadblocks and I could walk on the beach and have a swim whenever I wanted. I took great care to avoid getting malaria – once bitten, twice shy.

During my stay a beggar approached me one day outside a shop and I noticed that he was an amputee, his arm having been amputated below the elbow.

'You're back,' he said. I looked at him, did not recognise him and thought that maybe the comment was part of his begging technique, but then he said, 'I was in Murraytown during the war when you were there,' and he smiled. 'How de bodi?' He asked.

'De bodi gud'.

This time, it was.

Mr Ray Would Like a Monkey

6

Mozambique

TRYING TIMES

The intervening time between leaving Sierra Leone in 1999 and my next posting was not as easy as I had hoped. I had enrolled for a course in Dublin to train as an Emergency Medical Technician (EMT). It seemed that just as I was making progress in my recovery from malaria, I was in for yet another setback. I had an accident in November on my motorbike, resulting in neck, shoulder and leg injuries, and was on crutches for nearly six months. But I had recovered sufficiently by the late summer of 2000 to accept a job in Mozambique, which had been devastated by floods. I thought that the posting would be easy-going development work, but within a very short time of arriving realised that the situation was not as simple or as easy-going as I had hoped.

A NEW EXPERIENCE

My flight was from Dublin to London, on to Johannesburg in South Africa, and from there on to Maputo, the capital of Mozambique. I was met at Maputo Airport by a Concern driver and driven into the city for an overnight stay at a Concern house. The next morning I was brought into the office and given a short briefing.

Prior to the flooding disaster there had already been a team in place, engaged in long-term development work, and additional people had been brought in to deal with the emergency. The fact that there was a team already based in Maputo was a huge advantage when dealing with the emergency phase, as all that was needed were additional emergency workers to supplement the existing staff.

I was introduced to the team by Mairead, an Irish nurse who oversaw several building projects involving schools. I was informed that I would be based in a town called Chokwe, which had been severely affected by the flooding. Along with Mairead I was driven to Chokwe and met Per, a Swedish engineer who oversaw the actual site work. He was close to my age and we hit it off, especially when he referred to Mairead as granny. She appeared to be incredibly young to have such a responsible position but then, to us old guys, everyone seemed very young.

Per outlined the work in progress and what was planned. The next day I travelled around with him to the various sites. He gave me some work to look after, measuring some buildings and preparing a schedule of work to be carried out on an existing school. The pace of work was steady and there was no pressure involved, something I realised I missed quite a bit.

During the second week, Per told me that he had to fly to a town called Beira, which was up on the coast. We had a regional office there that had been set up to support quite an extensive building programme out in the bush. There was a sub-office in a place called Buzi, where the building team were based from Monday to Friday, but it was almost a four-hour drive from Beira.

Per was gone for a few days and when he came back he seemed a bit preoccupied. 'Granny is coming up to see us,' he said, and I thought nothing of it.

However, when Mairead arrived she immediately started a discussion about the Beira project. She explained to me that there was still a lot of work outstanding and that time was running out. Funding for the projects had been guaranteed from the EU, provided that all the work was completed by 30 October. It was now the first week in September and the work on building two new schools that were included in the funding was just starting, but using direct labour. The rest of the package included major renovations on several other schools, as well as building latrines. This was being carried out by building contractors, but all work needed careful supervision by us.

The supervisory staff consisted of an English engineer, Ann, and two local engineers, both of whom were very young and just a few years qualified.

'How would you feel about going up to Beira and giving a hand out?' Mairead asked.

'It would involve living out in the bush during the week and going back to Beira for the weekends.'

I didn't have to think about it. It was just what I needed, a challenge – and out in the bush all week, as well. Just what I liked! She explained that Ann was due to go on leave for a week, but that she would brief me before she left.

We went back from Chokwe to Maputo for the weekend and on Monday morning I went to the airport for my flight to Beira. Mairead had said that she would be up in a few days to see how I was getting on. I was really looking forward to the new project and so was not prepared for the reception that I received when I arrived.

BEIRA

I was met at the airport by Maryann, known as Ma'an, and Viktor. Ma'an was part of the international staff and Viktor was the local logistician. All supplies for the new schools had to be sourced and delivered through the Beira office. I was driven to the office and met the local accountant, Inez, who dealt with all financial matters.

I was informed that we had the use of two houses, one of which was used for an office and the other was for living in. There were drawings and bills of quantities (BOQs) sitting on a desk and I was told that they were for me. BOQs are a schedule of all the work required for a particular project and give a description of each item, the quantity involved and the cost. I had a quick look through them and, although they were in Portuguese, I was impressed at the professional way they had been prepared. When I asked where Ann was, I was told that she was in the house across the road. Ma'am then brought me to the house and led me up the stairs to a door. I knocked on the door and informed Ann that I had arrived and asked if we could meet soon. I was looking forward to getting a briefing and so was quite surprised when she said that she was not coming out to see me.

When I asked what the problem was she told me that she had been working extremely hard and now I had been sent up to take over her projects. I tried to calm things down, complimented her on the drawings and BOQs and said that I was there to assist her and that she was in charge, but all to no avail.

I thought that it was best to let matters rest for a while and told her through the door that I was going over to the office and maybe we could meet in the morning, but she shocked me even more by saying that she was going to the airport early in the morning and wouldn't be back. I went back to the office and phoned Mairead in Maputo who told me that while I was travelling up to Beira, Ann had given in her notice. She was travelling to England and was not returning.

I then learned that almost six months previously Ann had come directly to Mozambique from Kosovo without a break and I felt a certain sympathy for her. Going from one emergency to another is not a good idea because eventually you just run out of steam. So it was that I took over a number of projects, all at different stages, without any discussion with my predecessor. This was not what I had expected.

BUZI

Our construction sub-office and accommodation were located in Buzi (pronounced Boozie), a journey of nearly four hours by road from Beira. It was now early in the afternoon and Viktor and Ma'an were going to Buzi in a pick-up with bags of cement and some reinforcing mesh. I thought that the sooner I got to

Buzi the better and so threw my bag in the back along with the supplies and jumped into the front of the pick-up, leaving us all a bit squashed.

The first half of the journey was on a smooth, hardtop road, but after that we had to turn off onto a dirt track that was full of potholes. Eventually we came to a building site where some men were digging out foundations.

'This is Bueni, and this is where we are going to build one of the new schools,' I was informed.

The cement and reinforcing mesh were handed over and I was introduced to the foreman. I had a quick look around and could see that the job was not far advanced, but said nothing.

Next we journeyed on and a while later passed a small village. A building on the left was pointed out to me and I was informed that it was another school that had been renovated after the floods by a contractor, but that there was still some work required before it was finished. They referred to it as Guarra Guarra.

Eventually we arrived in Buzi and drove straight to a girls' secondary school complex where there was a lot of building activity. Ma'an introduced me to a young man named Joseph and told me that he was my interpreter. Joseph brought me over to another young man and introduced him as Michael, who I discovered was one of our civil engineers. I was glad to hear that he had a good command of English. He told me that the work at the school was being carried out by a contractor and so our presence was required intermittently on-site to ensure that the work was up to standard and to deal with any queries that might arise.

'I am glad that you are here,' Michael said, and I felt welcome, if not a little apprehensive. I reassured him that my job was to help, but that before we got down to specifics, I would like to see all the sites so that I would have a better understanding of all that was involved.

I had not expected to find myself in the thick of things from day one, but it looked like that was what I would have to deal with. Michael showed me around the site and then brought me to yet another school, which turned out to be a boys' boarding school where roof repairs were being carried out, as well as the installation of some electric lighting and the construction of new latrines. This work was also being carried out by a contractor. I could see that this was a busy set-up.

HOME SWEET HOME

Next he informed me that our living accommodation was close by and within a few minutes we had arrived at our cottage. Buzi was very unusual for a small African town. Previously its main source of income had been farming and then processing sugar cane at a large factory, but the sugar factory was no longer in operation and the surrounding fields were covered in weeds.

The town was laid out on a grid pattern, something that really surprised me, and the grid ended abruptly at the banks of the Buzi River. However, on a much smaller scale on the far side of the river, was a traditional African village. We were based on the grid side of the river and I had a quick look around the town that first evening.

I was delighted to see thick green vegetation growing on each side of the dirt track – this was what I liked. It looked like the greenery was trying to swallow the road.

Our base was a small bungalow with a tin roof with walled gardens front and back. In the front garden was a large tree. At the back was a veranda that ran the full width of the house and this would be my haven when I had time to sit and read in the evenings.

The accommodation consisted of a small kitchen, a living area, two bedrooms and a bathroom. I was shown into one of the bedrooms where a number of mattresses were stacked against the wall and several mosquito nets hung from the ceiling.

'This is where you will sleep. The house is not big enough for all of us, so we have a few tents in the garden and some of the team sleep out there,' explained Michael.

The resident team, as I discovered, consisted of the two engineers, several foremen, drivers and a logistician, while the rest of the construction team was recruited locally. There was a housekeeper who lived nearby and looked after our meals and washing.

In the living area was a large table that doubled as a desk when not being used for meals. The cooking was done on a gas cooker and we had a generator in the yard that provided electric light and a few sockets. My first impressions were good, it was homely. Dinner was served a short time later and, if not delicious, was at least palatable.

I was conscious that my sudden presence could be intimidating for the team and just gave my little pep talk about being there to help and told them that in the evening time, they should just do what they normally did to pass the time, which I discovered mostly involved chatting up the local girls. All this information was passed on through Joseph, the interpreter. I could see, however, that they were somewhat intimidated and maybe suspicious of my presence and realised that I was going to have to win them over. As it turned out they quickly came around, once I was able to solve a few outstanding issues, and we established a routine that they could relate to, but the first few weeks were quite stressful for us all.

SITE VISITS

Sunrise came just after 6 a.m. every morning, but the cock crowing out in the garden seemed to feel that he should have us all awake before the sun had actually crept over the horizon. I had a quick wash and after breakfast we left for the various sites.

I had asked Michael to take charge of the site visits to make the best use of our time.

'We will not go to Muchinessa today,' he said, referring to a site on the opposite side of the river. 'It takes too long, and it would be better to see as much as possible on this side.'

Instead, Peter, the second engineer, would go there on his own, as there were several issues to be resolved.

However, before we could go to any sites, I had to pay a courtesy visit to the local official who was responsible for the efficient running of the town. I was told that it would be very rude to go anywhere without informing the official of my presence and asking him to agree to my having freedom of movement in his area. Although this was a formality, it was important to acknowledge his authority and so off we went to the far side of the town. Michael and Joseph accompanied me and after a friendly cup of tea and a chat, I left with the clear understanding that I had the official's support, but that he would be keeping an eye on me and on what we were doing.

BUZI GIRLS' SECONDARY SCHOOL

We headed over first to the girls' secondary school in Buzi, where we checked in with the builder and Michael then gave me a guided tour.

On the existing school building, sheeting was being stripped off the roof in preparation for new roofing. The mosquito netting on the windows had to be replaced and electrical wiring was going to be installed. There was a small local electrical power supply but very few buildings were connected to it. Michael pointed out that lighting and some sockets would be installed so computer skills could be taught. When I questioned the need for lighting he surprised me by saying that the school would be in use from 8 a.m. until 10 p.m. each day and that at the weekends the school was used as a community centre. Different age groups attended classes at different times during the day and adult education was run at night-time, so the school was in constant use.

I was impressed by this efficiency and reminded of a poster that I had seen some years before in Dublin, which read: 'I went to Africa to teach and was surprised by how much I learned.'

The builder was making good progress and there seemed little to be concerned about, but Murphy's law (whatever can go wrong, will go wrong) never misses an opportunity. That opportunity would not be long in presenting itself.

BUENI

Next we journeyed up the road to Bueni, where we had been the previous day and where we were building the new school using direct labour. It was very hot, and I sat down with Michael in the shade of a tree to have some lunch I had brought with me. I noticed that part of the foundation for the new school had been filled back in with clay and when I asked Michael why this was, I was told that the education authority had decided that the school would be too close to the dirt track road and so they had altered the overall location of the school.

'Better to discover that now than when the school is built,' was my reply, and he seemed somewhat relieved. I wondered if he was thinking that I would be blaming him, as the engineer, for not setting out the building correctly.

After the quick lunch we had a walk around the site and the foreman seemed a bit agitated as he spoke to Michael. I didn't want to get sucked into everyday issues at that stage, but when Michael told me that there were a few issues that needed dealing with, I asked him to explain. The foreman was pointing at the bags of cement stacked nearby and waving his arms about.

'He says there is not enough cement for the rest of the foundation,' Michael said.

'Some was delivered yesterday when you came down from Beira, but it is not enough. Viktor went back to Beira this morning and will get more cement, but he won't be back until tomorrow sometime, so we will be held up.'

I could understand the foreman's frustration.

I enquired if we had a stockpile of cement and was told we hadn't and that it was delivered in the pick-up as required.

'OK,' I said, 'we can sort out that problem, not today, but I will get it sorted. Anything else?'

'Yes, water is a big issue. There is a well and pump nearby, which was installed by an NGO a few years ago and it provided enough fresh water for the village, but when we put in the first part of the foundations we took so much water out of the well for mixing the concrete that the well nearly ran dry. The villagers have told us not to use the pump anymore.'

I could see a few barrels of water close by and enquired about them.

'That water came from a river close by,' I was told. 'We drive the pick-up down to the river and fill the barrels using buckets, so getting water takes up a lot of time.'

'Anything else?' I enquired.

'Yes, we also use the pick-up to get sand from a pit some distance away and so when the pick-up is there, we cannot get water from the river, so the situation is not good. We have just started work in Muchinessa as well and if the pick-up is going to be used for transporting goods for Muchinessa the situation will be even worse.'

It was obvious that we needed another pick-up. I was getting the picture, but he had another surprise for me.

'We have a team for breaking the stones, but we need to speed it up. It takes a long time to break the stones so we need to increase the number of men now or we will be held up further down the road.'

Breaking stones on-site was a new concept to me.

At this stage I believe a technical explanation is required. Concrete consists of cement, sand and aggregate (stones) plus a considerable amount of water. If it is reinforced, then steel bars or mesh are placed into the wet concrete. However, the aggregate is sized or graded from small stones up to larger stones in such a way that there are no voids in the finished product. The smaller stones fill up the gaps between the larger stones and with the addition of the sand and the cement and water, the resultant concrete should be a solid mass, with no voids, as voids weaken the finished product.

I was informed that there were no small stones or aggregate readily available, as there was no commercial company supplying them, and so we had to break the large ones down physically, using hammers. This was very labour-intensive and took a lot of time. I now knew that I still had a lot learn about the local way of

Mr Ray Would Like a Monkey

doing things. I turned to Michael and thanked him for clarifying the situation and then told him that really what we had were several issues of a logistical nature, which were solvable.

'We should make arrangements to recruit more men for stone-breaking. What do you think?'

He agreed and told the foreman to arrange what was needed.

'Anything else?' I asked

'Yes, bricks. We have received a small amount, but we need lots more very soon and they can't deliver in time.'

In the middle of these discussions Peter, the second engineer, had arrived on the site on a small motorbike and had overheard the discussion. I asked Joseph to ask him what the story in Muchinessa was.

'Similar situation. Although water is not a problem there, transport is, as suppliers will not drive their trucks down the road, as they risk damaging them,' Joseph replied.

I had written down all the immediate problems and had some solutions in my head, but the big question was, would I be able to get the additional resources that I needed to solve the problems – and within the time required. One thing was certain, finishing the two schools in the allotted seven weeks was impossible, but even with an extra month added it would be tough going.

Mairead was due to visit in a few days and I was going to have to lay it all on the line to her.

My plan was that I would go to Muchinessa first thing in the morning and bring my team of Joseph my interpreter and the two engineers with me. After that I would call a meeting and hear what the team had to say.

As some of the guys sat in the house that evening I could detect an air of despondency, so I said little. I told Joseph not to hang about on my account and he went off down the village. I decided to go for a walk on my own and to explore the village a bit. There were a couple of local bars around and I could see some of our guys chatting up the girls. Someone was having a good time.

MUCHINESSA

Early the next morning I was down at the jetty on the river, along with Joseph and the engineers. The place was a hive of activity, with boats going back and forth. There were two ways to get to the site. The quickest way was to go downriver by boat and then disembark onto the riverbank. The river, however, was in tidal flow, so if the tide was out, it was a bit of a struggle to get up the slippery riverbank. Once on dry land, there was then a walk of about twenty minutes before we arrived at the site.

The other way of travelling was to cross the river by boat in a straight line from the jetty and disembark onto another jetty on the opposite side. This was a lot easier than the riverbank expedition, but the drawback was that it took over an hour to drive to the site on the rutted dirt track that curved inland before curving back out towards the river. There was a market held each morning near the far jetty. As the weeks passed I grew to love the atmosphere there whenever we travelled that route. There were stalls with all sorts of stuff and I would become their best customer when it came to buying bananas.

While Bueni had the advantage of being on the relatively good road, Muchinessa had the distinct disadvantage that from a logistical point of view it seemed to be in the middle of nowhere. When I enquired about its strange location I was told that in fact it had been accessible before the flooding, but that several bridges had been washed away, thereby cutting it off.

One or two suppliers were willing to deliver from Beira to Muchinessa, but it took six to eight hours to get there, assuming the rains had not arrived. The weather was another issue that had to be factored in as, according to the locals, the rains would start in November and when that happened the road to Muchinessa was practically impassable. It was another situation that had to be considered when organising our deliveries.

When I arrived at the Muchinessa site, having boated down the river and walked across some farmland, a situation similar to Bueni greeted me. I listened to Peter, Michael and the foreman explain the problems. Joseph, to his credit, just interpreted when he had to but did not get involved in the technical issues. Michael's English was good and although Peter and I could understand one another, I was careful to have Joseph interpret what Peter and the foreman said, just to avoid any misunderstanding.

We made our way back from Muchinessa towards Buzi, not by boat this time but along the road, as I wanted to see it first-hand. It was deeply rutted, with some ruts over a foot deep. When we arrived back at the river we got a boat across to the other side, after which we drove up the road towards Bueni.

We stopped at the school in Guarra Guarra that had recently been renovated. The contractor had done a good job, but there were still latrines to be built and there was no one on-site. We went off to look for the builder and found him at a different site. After I was introduced to him we discussed finishing off the contract. He was a huge man and must have weighed over 25 stone. He was full of chat but reluctant to confirm when he would be back on our site. I thought that it was not a big issue compared to the other problems that needed sorting, but our two engineers said that we would have to keep after him.

THE FIRST EVENING MEETING

Throughout my working life in the construction industry, it had always been my practice to ask people to be clear about not only the problems they saw, but also the solutions. My mantra was: identify the problem, identify the solution, identify the cost, identify who pays.

If issues were addressed in this sequence, solutions could be found without getting distracted about the cost or who was liable for it. I shared this with the team through Joseph and saw that one or two were interested, but others seemed reluctant to get involved. I informed them that I was taking over and asked them to tell me their problems. Michael, who had spent the most time with me since I had arrived, spoke to the team in Portuguese and when they still seemed reluctant to engage, I decided to take the bull by the horns.

'Cement,' I said, 'I hear that you are running short at times, why?'

Joseph translated into Portuguese and a three-way conversation started. When I spoke in English Joseph translated for the team, and when the team answered in Portuguese, Joseph translated into English.

Michael answered by saying that the deliveries were in small quantities, as it was delivered in the pick-up and they were now using it faster than it was arriving.

'How much do you feel that we need to have in stock to keep us going for the next month?' I asked.

'Thirty tonnes would be good,' replied Michael.

'Have we storage facilities?' I asked, and Michael said that we had.

'Enough space for 30 tonnes?'

'Yes,' he replied.

'Ok, get on the radio and order 30 tonnes of cement tomorrow, fill out the supply request and I'll sign it. Tell Viktor to hire a 30-tonne truck and get the cement down here without delay.'

'Viktor won't agree to that, he's in charge of supplies.' I was told.

'No,' I said, 'Viktor's job is to get the supplies that I authorise and to deliver them in the timeframe that you need them. Otherwise you cannot do your job.'

I enquired if we had storage facilities in Bueni and was told that we had.

'The truck will have to go through Bueni on the way down here so get them to drop half the load there and bring the rest to Buzi. We will store the cement here and arrange to get it transferred across the river to Muchinessa.'

Joseph translated for the team and I could see a few faces getting a bit more interested as they discussed it among themselves.

'Next,' I said, 'water in Bueni. What we need is a big water storage facility. There are tanks called fastanks that are used in emergencies. They are made of polythene sheeting and come in a kit with supporting rails. When water is put into them the weight of the water stabilises them and they have capacity of several thousand litres. If we can get a water pump we can fill the barrels much more quickly than at present and then pour the water from the barrels into the tank and just top it up as required, once we have it nearly full. That will leave more time for using the pick-up for getting sand to the site.'

I asked Michael and Peter what they thought of my suggestion and they seemed enthusiastic. They thought that we needed extra transport for a number of weeks, and I agreed. We were reaching the same conclusions, which I found reassuring. We decided that we would request another two pick-ups and drivers from Mairead.

Next we moved on to the supply of bricks and this was down to the brick manufacturer in Beira. There was a big demand for bricks and there was a waiting list for orders to be processed. We agreed that we would visit the brickworks after the weekend and see what could be arranged, but I was bit worried because without bricks we would come to a standstill.

I told the team that I could see that they were frustrated but pointed out that I would work hard to try and sort out the supply issues. You will have all the cement you want very soon, and I will work with the engineers to sort out the water as quickly as possible. I told them that making the necessary changes was like trying to turn a big ship around. It would take time, but once we got going in the right direction, it would get a lot easier.

'Give me two weeks to get things sorted,' I asked.

THE LOCAL BAR

I enquired about the nearest place to go for a drink. It was still extremely hot and after the meeting I was led to a timber-built shop and bar that had white plastic chairs and tables. I offered to buy some beer for the team and discovered that the routine, when there was a group of people, was for just a few one-pint bottles of beer to be ordered. We were each given a small glass and when the bottles were opened the contents were shared.

After the guys had relaxed a bit, Michael said that looking after the main contractors had been all right, but because of the supply issues for the new schools, he had been losing heart and had considered quitting. I was a bit shocked and realised that without him I would be under terrible pressure, as he was obviously the most knowledgeable of the team when it came to local building methods and I could see that the men respected him.

I asked him to give me the few weeks to get matters sorted and promised that I would involve him and Peter in making decisions. I was going to have to work really hard to get the ship going in the right direction.

MAIREAD

The next morning I had a quick discussion with the engineers about the time frame required for the two schools and using a bar chart we worked out a rough programme. A bar chart is a planning tool that lists all the major operations in the building programme and sets a time frame for each. It is normally drawn up on graph or squared paper in a table format. A series of squares, each representing a week, are drawn across the top of the chart, while down the left-hand side of the page, a brief description of each main procedure is listed. The list is made in the sequence of the building operations – for example, excavating the foundations is followed on the next line by concreting the foundations.

We listed all the main operations in sequence and then allocated time for each, filling in one box for each week of work required. By following this procedure we could estimate how many weeks it should take to construct the schools, after which we could fine-tune the chart, where operations could overlap.

It was even more obvious from the chart that the two schools, assuming that we had all the materials and support required, could not be built in the time allocated, of just under two months. In fact it would require careful coordination to have the buildings finished in almost three months. I could see why Michael was beginning to feel that he was on mission impossible.

Mr Ray Would Like a Monkey

When Mairead arrived I informed her that we needed to sort out a lot of issues without delay. I told her about the supply problems and the unworkable time frame and asked her why the programme had not been started sooner. I could understand why Ann had felt that she'd had no option but to call it a day.

Mairead explained that there was a certain amount of funding for the work, but that when it came to the two new schools, the Ministry of Education had been insisting that teacher accommodation had to be built at each school. The reasoning behind this was that it was very hard to recruit teachers for Bueni and Muchinessa, but if accommodation was provided, it would be easier. The funding, however, did not cover accommodation, so a large part of the time allocated for construction had been used up waiting for an agreement. Ann could not order materials if the projects were not going ahead. She had had enough. I sympathised, but it was my problem now. Various issues needed to be sorted out quickly and Mairead would have a major part to play in the sorting.

A NEW PLAN

I explained to Mairead that with a one-month extension the work could just about be done, but only if we had certain facilities immediately. These included an additional two pick-ups and drivers, as well as a water pump and an emergency fastank for the length of the contract. I explained about the well having been almost run dry in Bueni.

In addition, we had yet to sort out the problem of brick deliveries and I requested permission to agree quicker payment terms than normal with the brick supplier. She agreed to all my requests and said that she would follow up straight away.

LOGISTICS

People can often feel that they are doing a good job because they are rushing around like mad, and this was the case with logistics in Beira. They were working hard. Viktor was rushing backwards and forwards between Beira and Buzi when what he should have been doing was organising matters from Beira. Spending a day collecting goods in Beira, driving to Buzi and offloading and then returning to Beira was not a good use of his time. When he was told to organise the truck for delivery of the 30 tonnes of cement, he argued that the truck would cost money, whereas he could deliver with the pick-up at no extra cost. I pointed out that if he delivered a half tonne of cement in the pick-up per day, it would take him 60 days to deliver 30 tonnes. Not only was this far too slow, but he would be unavailable for other work. He didn't seem to get it, but we insisted that a large truck was used for this job. I had not made a friend. Next I explained that we needed a fastank and he should make enquiries to see where we could get one. I was pleasantly surprised when he replied that we already had one in the store in Beira! Ann had obviously anticipated the need for such an item and had arranged it. I wished that she was there so that I could thank her. We decided that the team would bring it down to Bueni after the weekend. Meanwhile, Mairead had made her way back to Beira and was working hard for us on all fronts.

THE WEEKEND

By the time I returned to Beira on Friday night I was a bit apprehensive. What if the extra support was not forthcoming or if the programme dates could not be extended? I needn't have worried. Mairead had contacted the Concern office in Chimoio, which was near the border with Zimbabwe, explained the situation and they had agreed to our request for two pick-ups and drivers, along with a water pump.

'They will be in Buzi sometime on Monday and we can have them for at least six weeks. I have requested a one-month extension on the contract and we'll have confirmation after the weekend, but it should be OK.'

I looked around and the fastank, which comes in a wooden box with all the necessary kit, was beside my desk in the office. Brilliant I thought, this is the sort of support we need.

Mr Ray Would Like a Monkey

Budgets

Getting the job done in time was not the only consideration, of course. Budgets had been set and the work had to be carried out within the amounts agreed.

Mairead and Inez, the accountant, sat down with me on Saturday morning and talked me though the figures. The renovations had all been quoted for by the builders and were well within budget. There was a budget for the two new schools being built with direct labour, but little of it had been used, so I would have to keep a careful eye on it. I asked Inez if she could give me a weekly running total of all costs for each project and she was happy to oblige. She promised me that I would have the up-to-date details on Monday morning each week before I departed for Buzi. I was impressed by her professionalism. I was given a copy of all the relevant budgets and put them in my file. I was starting to get a feel for the job, although I was still a bit shocked at the idea that I was in charge.

Bricks

First thing on Monday morning, I sat down with Michael and Joseph and, using the bar chart as a guide, we worked out an approximate delivery schedule for the bricks for both schools, based on the revised programme. We were putting Mairead under pressure with all our demands, but sometime later she came back to us to say that she had got an extension, but only up to 30 November and not a day more.

'We must be finished, and all the accounts agreed by then,' she said.

'Brilliant!' I thought, as we turned our minds back to sorting out the brick supply problem.

We did not need a full delivery of bricks in one go but required a steady flow and so split up the orders for both schools into several parts. The brickworks was not that far away and as we headed over to their office we were all a bit worried.

Joseph did the introductions in his role as interpreter and explained why we were there. I explained about the funding arrangements and that we had time constraints, but the manager was not too sympathetic.

'We have lots of orders and are very busy,' he said.

There were hundreds of thousands of bricks stacked up on pallets out in the yard and I pointed out that not all the bricks there would be used in the next few weeks. I suggested that if we borrowed a small percentage from several of the big orders that were stacked in the yard, he could get us moving, and when the bricks for our order were ready, they could be given to the customers we had borrowed from.

'If you can quicken up delivery for us, maybe we could quicken up payment to you,' I said. That got his interest.

Most commercial contractors were working on credit of several months. We, on the other hand, had funds available and did not have to wait to pay our bills. I suggested that if he could meet our delivery schedule, we could pay the company for each delivery within a week or so and that would be a very good cash flow for him. If, on the other hand, we could not get delivery in time, we might have to defer the building. I told him that the delivery dockets could be back in Beira each Friday night and that if his invoice was in our office and matched the docket, I would sign it off for payment for the following week. Now he had a good reason to deliver quickly.

I had discussed the quick payment approach with Inez before negotiating and she had told me that there would not be a problem, provided that I told her a week or two in advance of when the payments would be required. I was reassured by all the cooperation. After a short time, we headed back to Buzi for what would become a ritual each week, the Monday night meeting when our plans for the week would be discussed. I was looking forward to the meeting. Mairead was going to travel with us down to Buzi.

Mr Ray Would Like a Monkey

TERMITES

We headed towards Buzi, stopping off at Bueni on the way. Peter had already travelled down during the morning with the rest of the team and so was in Bueni when we pulled in. The team had quickly got to grips with the fastank and had it erected on the site. We told Peter about the proposed meeting in the house after dinner that evening and that we had good news.

We then headed on to Buzi where the contractor's men were just about finishing up for the day at the girls' secondary school. As soon as we pulled up, the builder approached Michael and told us that there was problem. I had been feeling quite happy after Beira, but my bubble was about to be burst.

The problem turned out to be something no one had anticipated. When all the old roof sheets had been removed it was noticed that quite a few rafters were very bent and looked unstable. Further investigation showed that there was a termite infestation and as a result all the rafters were structurally unsound. The builder wanted to know what we wanted to do. I conferred with Michael, who explained that termites eat the centre out of the timber until it becomes so weak that it collapses. I was glad to have all this local knowledge available to me and agreed that the timbers would have to be replaced, but before we did that we needed a quote and I also had to look at the budget.

The builder had anticipated the need for the quote and had a figure already worked out, but when I checked in my file I realised that we were going to go over budget. However, I was also aware, after my discussion with Inez, that some of the other jobs that were almost complete would come in under budget.

Mairead was standing beside me and looking worried and I asked her if the budgets were individual for each project or if it was possible to use savings from one to top up another.

'They are transferrable,' she said, 'so long as the total overall figure doesn't exceed what's been agreed.'

Just what I wanted to hear!

We told the builder to replace the rafters, but at the same time drew a line in the sand.

'You can collect the order in the morning for the extra work, but just remember, we only pay for any changes if there is an order issued and signed by us before you carry out the work.'

I did not want him to think that I was going to be soft on charges for any extra work.

Monday night meeting

The first Monday night meeting that we held was, to my mind, the ship starting to turn. It was held immediately after dinner, as in this way nobody could escape to chase the local girls before we got started.

I was keen to involve everybody on the team but noticed that the drivers were not present and when I enquired about them was told that they were not normally involved in discussions. I insisted that they be brought into the meeting. I could see that there was a bit of a hierarchy involved and to the tradespeople the drivers were of little significance, so I laid it on the line. 'We are all part of a team and each of you has a part to play,' I informed them.

'But the drivers don't build anything,' one of the men said.

'No, but without them, you would not be able to do your job. They bring you to and from work, collect the sand and water, deliver other items as required and when we start to build in Muchinessa, the drivers will be a major part of making sure that you get deliveries of materials to that site. Without the drivers the job will come to a stop. They are to be at all future meetings.'

This was not what they were used to, I could see, but they went and brought the drivers in. I told them about the fastank in Bueni and that a water pump had been delivered. In addition, brick deliveries had been agreed. The two new drivers from Chimoio were then introduced to the team.

'From now on, each Monday evening after dinner, we will plan the work for the week and a schedule for visits to the different sites will be agreed,' I said.

One issue that had been apparent was the amount of time that was involved in getting to and from the Muchinessa site, and prior to the meeting I had discussed the matter with Peter and Michael. I suggested that Peter be resident on that site only, as it needed a lot of supervision. He was more than happy to agree and so I informed the team of the new arrangement.

The bricks would be delivered by the supplier to the new schools in Bueni and Muchinessa. The suppliers of other goods, such as timber and cement refused to travel on the bad roads to Muchinessa, so we would have to deliver those goods onwards after they had been delivered to the store in Buzi. I told them that one of the new pick-ups would be going to Muchinessa the next day and would be based there, along with the one already on-site. The plan was to transport most of the materials in storage from Buzi down to the jetty and then by boat across the river to the landing dock on the far side. The pick-ups on the far side would then deliver the goods to the site. The logisticians would coordinate the delivery and would liaise with Peter on-site. When the new driver asked how to get to Muchinessa, he was given directions. When he asked how long it would take, I was shocked to hear that the answer was eight to ten hours. I thought they were joking until it was explained that several bridges had been washed away in the floods.

Next we came to the discussion about the new school in Bueni. The sourcing of the fastank and pump seemed to have impressed some of the team and the importance of the role of the drivers soon became obvious. One driver and his team were made responsible for filling the barrels with water from the river, now using the pump, and transporting the barrels to the site where they would transfer the water into the fastank. Michael had marked a piece of wood with maximum and minimum levels of water required in the tank. When the maximum level was reached the driver would take the team off to collect sand, and each time he returned he would check on the level of the water. When it was down near the minimum level, he would switch the team back to collecting water and suspend the sand deliveries.

When the driver asked who would tell him when to switch, I told him that he would make the decision.

'You are in charge of water and sand, so it is your responsibility. You and your team are very important. Without sand or water the job will stop. All of the communication on my part was translated by Joseph, of course, but when the driver puffed up his chest, smiled at the others around the table and said something in Portuguese that made them laugh, I asked Joseph what had been said.

'Mr Ray says I am very important, and I have never been told that before, I am very happy to be here with you all', replied Joseph.

I decided to quit while I was ahead and asked them if they would like to go for a drink in the local bar. When we arrived at the little pub that I had been in the previous week I asked Joseph to order for me. Small glasses were set up for us all and the ritual of pouring the contents of one bottle into several glasses was performed and we raised our glasses to one another. I was beginning to feel at home.

Lost in translation

The BOQ for each job was printed on one side of an A4 sheet of paper and held together to form a small booklet, all written in Portuguese of course, but with Joseph's help I had written on the opposite page the descriptions of the main work in English. This way I could see what the Portuguese was for various items, such as cement and timber and nails and I made a special effort to use the Portuguese words when referring to the different items on-site and at our meetings. My attempts were well received, and I noticed that several of the team were more adept at English than I had realised. They attempted to use English at the Monday night meetings and I made an effort to use Portuguese. I was surprised at how much I was picking up. But one incident brought home to me the dangers of assuming too much, and things getting 'lost in translation' became a reality. The mood had lightened over the weeks and there was now a fair amount of laughing and joking. On one particular Monday evening I was trying to begin the weekly meeting but there were several discussions going on all at the same time. Joseph, sitting beside me, was deeply engrossed in his own storytelling. Suddenly there was a screeching sound outside the house and I said to Joseph, 'That sounds like a monkey.'

Joseph obviously misheard me and said, 'You would like a monkey?'

'No, that noise outside sounded like a monkey,' I replied.

From the other end of the table I heard someone speaking in Portuguese and just caught 'Mr Ray' and 'monkey', and there were smiles all around. I reckoned that I was on the receiving end of some joke and just laughed along with them.

At the meeting, all the week's plans were agreed, and we then followed our ritual of adjourning to the local pub, where we had our few beers. The mood had lightened on the sites and I was enjoying the atmosphere.

The following evening we were having our dinner and the bilingual chat was going back and forth around the table. I was enjoying the banter when there was a loud knock on the door.

'I wonder who that is?' I said to Joseph, and he just smiled and said, 'That is the man with the monkey.' The guys around the table laughed and I laughed along with them. However, when the door opened and a stranger came in with a spider monkey on a lead, I nearly fell off the chair.

'What's going on?' I asked and Joseph replied, 'You said that you would like a monkey, so this man has brought a monkey for you. We sent for him so that you could have company. She is tame and is a pet.' All the guys were laughing and clapping, and I thought this had to be a wind-up.

'Pay the man,' he said, and I shook my head. I was still sure that it was a wind-up.

'You have to pay him,' said Joseph. 'He has walked for hours to get here and it would not be fair to send him away without paying him'.

Meanwhile the monkey had come over to us and lifted one arm in the air and I was told that she wanted to be scratched.

I scratched it and I was hooked as she held out her hand and waved it up and down. The owner spoke to Joseph, who then informed me that the monkey was looking for bananas. I handed over the requested money to the now ex-owner, who told us that the monkey's name was Chica. The monkey had a belt around its waist with a ring on it, and a rope threaded through the ring.

'Where are we going to keep it?' I enquired and Joseph pointed at the big tree in the garden.

'It can live up there,' he said, 'and after a week or so, we can let it off the rope. Once we feed the monkey, it won't wander off.'

I suggested that we set it free but was told that other monkeys would kill it as it was on its own. We tied the rope to a branch on the tree and the monkey shimmied up into it. After a week we removed the rope, but it didn't leave the garden. Bananas were purchased from the market across the river each day, either by me or one of the team working in Muchinessa. Each evening when I came back into the garden Chica would scramble up onto the bonnet of the Land Cruiser and hold out her hand for the bananas.

Most evenings when I had some spare time, I sat out on the veranda and read a book, and Chica would come and sit on the floor beside me. Sometimes when she was tired she would lie across my feet and go to sleep. One evening she was sitting on the low wall that surrounded the veranda and suddenly started screeching and jumping up and down. I looked up from my book to see what had her excited and suddenly saw a snake moving across the garden, just a few feet away. I sat still and within a few seconds it had gone out of the garden and I breathed a sigh of relief. I had seen several snakes around and was still surprised at how fast they could move. Now at least we had our own early warning system in the monkey.

WEEKENDS

I was really enjoying living in Buzi during the week. We were working extremely hard, but the team had a great sense of humour and we were definitely making progress. They were

Mr Ray Would Like a Monkey

happy that the bar chart had been stuck up on the wall in the house and the information on it was there for everyone to see. Joseph had written up the various tasks in Portuguese and had prepared a second chart for me in English. I was pleased to see them regularly checking the chart to make sure that they were not forgetting anything important.

I wrote up a progress report at the end of each week and this, along with the bar chart, formed the basis for our discussions at the Monday night meetings. Mairead, back again in Maputo, had to send in regular progress reports to the donors and I would send her the details for the donor reports when required.

The supervisors and engineers who lived in Beira would leave Buzi and Muchinessa on Friday afternoon to return home for the weekend, and I would travel with them. On Saturday morning I would get up early and start on the various reports that had to be prepared. The reports for Mairead would give details of all the work in progress by the contractors as well as our direct labour teams, and included costs to date, any issues that might be of concern, and our plans to deal with them. Inez, the accountant, was always on top of the finance reports and just passed the information on to me.

The reports for our own construction team only included the details of the construction of the two schools being built by direct labour in Bueni and Muchinessa. It would take a few hours on Saturday morning to get the reports finalised, after which I would send a few personal emails or take myself off to the beach, which was nearby. Sundays were for resting and, to be honest, a bit boring.

I missed the camaraderie that had developed with the team in Buzi and I looked forward to getting back to the team house there. We had arranged for Chica to be fed at the weekend by some of the locals and when we returned each Monday, we got a great welcome as she jumped up and down in the garden, obviously happy to see us.

On the first weekend after we had got her, I sat down in the Beira office to check emails as usual. Word had obviously spread fast and there were several emails from Mairead. I was reminded in no uncertain manner of the terms of my work contract. 'NO HOUSEHOLD PETS,' she wrote. 'I hear you have a monkey!'

'I do not have a household pet,' I wrote, 'it lives in the tree in the garden.'

When Mairead met Chica, it didn't take long to win her over.

I always slept well in Buzi, but the same could not be said for Beira. If Chica was our early warning system for snakes, our neighbour in Beira went one better and had installed about half a dozen turkeys in the garden. If anyone came close to the house the turkeys kicked up an unmerciful racket. I never got a full night's sleep when I was in Beira. I was much happier out in the bush.

ZIMBABWE

One weekend, while speaking with Inez and Ma'an, I discovered that before I had arrived, they had made several trips to Zimbabwe and spent the weekend there. They asked if I would mind driving there and I was more than happy to oblige. I was running low on books and needed reading material in English. I checked with Mairead to see if it was OK for me to take the car over the border and got the go-ahead straight away.

'All you have to do is bring your passports and the vehicle registration documents with you and pay for the fuel,' she said, and we were more than happy with that.

So the following week, I prepared the weekly reports early and emailed them from the office when I arrived back in Beira on Friday evening. I was looking forward to something different for the weekend. We set off early on Saturday morning for what was about a four-hour trip. The climate in Mozambique was very hot and sticky due to the high humidity but as we approached the border I could start to feel a difference. It was a nice warm day, but the humidity had reduced considerably and was very comfortable.

Mr Ray Would Like a Monkey

Ma'an had arranged accommodation for us in the town of Mutare, in an area called Leopard Rock. We went to the hotel and booked in before we headed into town for a look around.

My first impression of Zimbabwe was that it was like Scotland on a warm day. It was green with lots of fir trees. The people spoke English and were friendly. We had our lunch in a small pub and then walked down by some shops. I was hoping to find a shop that would have some books and couldn't believe my luck when I came across a shop called Kingston's Book Shop. A sign on the door showed that Visa credit cards were accepted, which was another plus. I told the girls that I would be a while and they wandered off to do their own shopping. I bought enough books to keep me going for a good few weeks and loaded them into my ever-present rucksack.

We had a lovely meal in the hotel that evening and the owner came and chatted with us for a while and explained that due to its elevation, Mutare was a very comfortable place to reside in. We finished off the evening in the small bar in the hotel and agreed that we would have to repeat the experience as soon as possible.

The next morning after breakfast we drove around the area and I was really taken with the feel of the place. I had found on previous occasions that sometimes I could arrive in a place and feel at home immediately, while other places took longer to adjust to. After the initial visit I managed to get a few more trips to Mutare and each time it felt like going on holiday.

MR CROCODILE

During the week in Buzi, I had a sort of routine where after my evening meal I would go for a short stroll and the locals would greet me as I walked around the town. They were probably thinking there goes the mad Irishman who has a monkey for company. The jetty at the river was a popular meeting place and sometimes Joseph would accompany me. On one particular evening we arrived at the jetty and as Joseph was having a chat with one of the locals I decided to take a rest. I sat down on the jetty and swung my legs over the side, my feet dangling a short distance above the water. The heat of the timber was seeping through my shorts and also into my hands and I was just thinking that it was a very relaxing and a lovely setting when Joseph suddenly roared at me.

'Get your feet up!' I was surprised and moved quickly. Then he explained.

'Crocodiles feed at dusk and dawn and there are many along the river. A boy was taken not too long ago and after the floods the crocodiles are scattered and all over the place. If he saw your feet dangling over the water, Mr Crocodile would have you for supper.'

It was the last time that I sat down at the jetty in the evening time.

MR FASTANK

The work was progressing steadily on most fronts and several of the jobs that were being carried out by contractors were nearing completion and within budget, I was glad to see. The young engineers had done a good job of supervising the builders. The only headache that seemed to drag on was the completion of the school near Guarra Guarra. The school was almost renovated but the work on the latrines had still not started.

When I had discussed this with Michael he suggested that we pay a visit to the builder again. I could not for the life of me pronounce the builder's name, but he was a huge man and one day without thinking I referred to him as Mr Fastank and the name stuck. We travelled to the site where he was working. When we approached him his modus operandi seemed to be to attack us verbally, me in particular. I was familiar with this technique, which was also used by builders back home. Make attack your defence.

Before we could discuss the matter of the latrines he demanded to know why I was not speaking in Portuguese.

'You are working in my country, so why are you speaking English?' he demanded.

'I work in many different countries,' I replied, 'and so, it is not practical to learn lots of different languages, especially as I have an interpreter. Anyway, I am only here for another few weeks and then I will return to Ireland and that is what will affect you, not me speaking English.' When he enquired what I meant, I explained that for him to receive the final payment on the job, I had to issue a certificate to say that the work was complete. 'If you have not completed the work before I leave, there will no one here to sign the certificate and you will have to wait for someone to come here from Maputo to check the work. The Beira office will be closing down at the end of the month.' That got his attention.

I asked him to explain what the difficulty was in starting the latrines. I knew from our own direct labour building team that the latrine construction, although a small part of the contract, was a little bit complicated, not least by the presence of a high-water table after the floods. I asked if he would have any objection to me taking the latrine construction out of his contract and getting someone else to do it, and he jumped at the offer. We had already discussed the possibility of extra work with the other builder, who was working in Buzi, and he said that he would be happy to take it on, as he did not have a lot of work lined up.

Mr Fastank quickly completed the outstanding items on the school and the second builder constructed the latrines. We were nearing completion of all the work being carried out by contractors and I was able to get the final accounts agreed, certificates issued and payment made without too much hassle.

THE HANDOVERS

As each school was completed, I was happy to hand them over and wish all involved the best of luck. I don't like fuss and prefer to get the job done and leave quietly, but this was not the plan that the authorities had in mind. Celebrations were prepared at each school and a big fuss made at each handover. Speeches were made and soft drinks and biscuits handed around. I had to make a speech on each occasion and Joseph would then translate and deliver it on my behalf. A few times there were bursts of laughter and I wondered if he was actually translating me or saying what he thought I should be saying.

As we ran down to the last few weeks I was busy with just the two schools that we were building by direct labour. The advantage with building by direct labour is that the costs are lower, but the work involved in planning and supervising is very time-consuming. Another side effect is that when a builder completes his contract, he clears the site of all surplus material, while on direct labour there is nowhere to remove it to. The engineers had asked me about this a while back and I thought that we might be able to solve two problems at once, so when we had discussed with the second contractor about taking over the latrine contract from Mr Fastank, I had offered a carrot.

I told the second builder that if he would build the latrines, we would pay him the same rate as he was paid before, but as he had to travel to Guarra Guarra each day, we would make him a special offer. This involved quantifying all the material left over at the two direct labour sites, valuing the goods using the supplier's invoices and then offering them to him at a good discount off the invoice value. He would not pay us for the goods directly, but rather we would deduct the amount off his final account. He was happy with the arrangement and so was I; it was a good agreement.

CLOSE-DOWN

The jobs were wrapped up and it was time to close the Buzi office. It was now the last week in November and we had just about made it timewise. All the schools were open, accounts agreed and the surplus materials were gone off site.

Per and Mairead had come to visit for the last few days to see the completed jobs. Mairead was happy and said so, but I had to say that without her help we would never have completed the work in such a short time.

'Teamwork is what got it done,' I said, 'and a monkey to keep an eye on us'.

It was a strange feeling slowing down after all the rushing around early on. Even the monkey looked a bit distracted, as if she was wondering what was going on. I wondered what I should

Mr Ray Would Like a Monkey

do with her, and even considered bringing her home, but didn't think that Liz would see that as a good idea. Joseph solved the problem, however, when he told me that he was going to open a small bar in Beira and asked if he could take Chica with him, as she might attract customers into the bar.

She won't survive on her own in the bush,' said Joseph, 'she has been a pet since she was very young.'

So we headed back to Beira for the last time, bringing Chica with us.

It only took a few days to complete the remaining paperwork in Beira. We handed back the office to the landlord and caught a plane to Maputo. Mairead was staying on in Maputo for a little longer, but for Per and me it was time to go. Per was also travelling to Ireland, so we travelled together and he stayed at my house for a few days. It was the beginning of December and it was good to be home, but I did miss the monkey.

A NEW YEAR

I worked in Dublin for almost eight months before another overseas offer came in. I was hoping that I would be going back to Africa and was a bit surprised when I was offered a position in Afghanistan. I had briefings in Dublin and was warned about the strict behavioural codes that existed in Afghanistan. I was not unduly worried and felt that it would be a new experience.

At the beginning of September, briefings complete, I was given my tickets. I was to fly to London, then Pakistan, and finally onwards to Afghanistan. My departure date was 11 September 2001, or 9/11, as it became known.

I left Dublin airport early that morning and made it as far as London before being recalled. It would be weeks before I finally got to Afghanistan. And that turned out to be a vastly different story.

7

The Last Word (by Liz)

'I've been offered a job.' How many times have I heard this since 1997? Not sure, but I would estimate about 25. The first time I heard this I was working in the reception area of a local business when the phone rang and Ray uttered those soon to be familiar words. At this stage I knew that he was interested in aid work and had been trying to find out how to get started in this field, so it wasn't a complete surprise when the call came that day. However, when I asked where this job was and Ray said Bosnia, it took me completely by surprise.

'Bosnia,' I whispered, having to think for a few seconds where Bosnia actually was.

Of course we had all seen and heard the news reports about the war in the Balkans and the terrible suffering of the civilians there, but that was far removed from our personal experience and now Ray was telling me that he was going out there. All sorts of questions rush through your mind at times like this, and I have learned over the years to let all these queries sit at the back of my mind for a few days before I articulate them. Of course I hadn't discovered this yet and I think I probably bombarded him with my questions and worries. However, I knew he wanted to do this type of work and, whatever my misgivings, I would not stand in his way.

Mr Ray Would Like a Monkey

We agreed that he should accept this posting and I secretly promised myself not to panic till after he had left.

Day of departure: off we went to the airport, parked the car and queued up at check-in (this was before the days of online check-in!). We waited around the departure area until the time came for him to go to the gate. I held it all together until this point, but when it came to the time of actually saying goodbye, we both got terribly upset. My mind was in turmoil with worry for Ray's safety first and foremost, and about how I would manage at home with him being so far away from home – all sorts of thoughts, I can't remember most of them!

Anyway, I watched him walk away through the gates and had to sit in the departures area for a while to regain my composure. In the last couple of years we have decided that this prolonged goodbye time is not a good idea, so now I drive Ray to the airport and drop him in the trolley area and drive off! You have to develop coping mechanisms.

During Ray's time in Bosnia communication was not as easy or instant as it is nowadays and it was a treat to get the occasional phone call, once from the balcony of a hotel in the city of Split in Croatia! Neither of us was computer-literate at the time and email was an unknown entity for us, so we were limited in the amount of communication we could have. While Ray was in South Sudan he wrote a few letters that were delivered to me by hand by other people returning from the area. One of them I remember was smudged by drops of sweat – he was writing in 45-degree heat. Occasionally I received a phone call via satellite phone from South Sudan, but this was expensive and not very satisfactory due to time delays on the line.

Following his return from Sarajevo, Ray travelled home with his boss at the time, Col. M Shannon, who stayed with us for a night before travelling on to his own home. In general conversation that evening he mentioned that, when he returned from a stressful job, he liked to have plenty of 'quiet time' to himself and not to have to answer questions from friends and family, no

matter how well meaning. I took this as a gentle hint as to how I should react to Ray.

It is not easy to return to normal family life after being away for long periods and it is also difficult for the person at home to re-adapt. While he was away I would probably make more of an effort to keep in touch with friends and family, even if a lot of them thought that he was quite mad.

Our children also had to adapt to their Dad being back home and did ask if I was happy for him to be away working in dangerous places. My answer to this was that if Ray was in the army or navy he would be away for even longer periods of time. That said, I do know that they are all proud of him and of the work he has done. When he returned from his first posting Ray realised how under-prepared he was to do aid work and set about getting the training he needed. Computer literacy was the first hurdle to overcome and many hours were spent puzzling over the keyboard. Also training in radio procedures, land mine awareness and other military stuff that I really didn't want to hear too much detail about! I think sometimes he enjoyed the training as much as the postings.

As mentioned before, returning from an overseas posting is difficult for both of us. If it has been a successful period then Ray is more relaxed and happier, but if there have been a lot of problems and difficult situations, he dwells on them and is more stressed. The nightmares he sometimes has can be very upsetting, and when something comes up on the radio or television he can get very emotional. It is extremely hard to put the suffering of children out of your mind, especially amputees or boy soldiers. Many people ask from time to time if this is his last job, or if he would go away again. Who knows? Never say never!

Liz Taylor

Mr Ray Would Like a Monkey